Little Bears
to knit & crochet

First published in paperback in Great Britain 2014

Search Press Limited
Wellwood, North Farm Road,
Tunbridge Wells, Kent TN2 3DR

First published in hardback in Great Britain in 2012

Based on material previously published in the 20 to Make
series as Knitted Bears All Dressed Up by Val Pierce, 2010;
and Crocheted Bears by Val Pierce, 2011

Text copyright © Val Pierce 2012
www.crossedneedles.co.uk

Photographs by Debbie Patterson at Search Press
Photographic Studio

Photographs and design copyright © Search Press Ltd 2012

ISBN PB: 978-1-78221-008-5
ISBN HB: 978-1-84448-756-1

The Publishers and author can accept no responsibility for
any consequences arising from the information, advice or
instructions given in this publication.

Readers are permitted to reproduce any of the items in this
book for their personal use, or for the purposes of selling for
charity, free of charge and without the prior permission of the
Publishers. Any use of the items for commercial purposes is
not permitted without the prior permission of the Publishers.

Suppliers

If you have difficulty in obtaining any of the materials and
equipment mentioned in this book, then please visit the Search
Press website for details of suppliers: www.searchpress.com

Acknowledgements

Many thanks to Coats Patons for their kind
donation of many of the yarns used to make the
knitted bears in this book, and to Sirdar, Patons
and DMC for kindly donating some of the yarns
needed to create the crocheted bears. Thank
you also to the team at Search Press for all their
hard work in putting this book together and to
the photographer, Debbie Patterson, for taking
the wonderful photographs. Last but by no
means least, a big thank you to my dear friends
and family for all their encouragement, patience
and inspiration.

Printed in China

Little Bears

to knit & crochet

Search Press

Contents

Crocheted Bears 52

Knitted Bears

Teddy bears have been a big favourite with both young and old for many, many years. Here I have created a set of charming little characters for you to knit. Each one has its own special outfit, right down to its tiny shoes. The bears measure just 8in (20cm) tall and and are knitted in simple garter stitch, taking just a few hours to make. You will only need small amounts of yarn to knit both the bears and the variety of clothes I have designed. Use up all the leftover yarns in your stash, and either follow my colour choices or use your imagination and make up your own. Whatever you decide to do, I am sure that you will be thrilled with the outcome.

Happy knitting to you all, and remember:

Your teddy bear's a treasure,
a comfort to behold.
He'll love you when you're tiny,
as well as when you're old.
He's always there to listen,
to lend a furry ear.
No matter how you treat him,
He'll always hold you dear.
Don't throw him in the corner,
or leave him on the mat,
always take him with you,
he'll be very pleased with that!

Basic knitting patterns

Bear

What you need

1 pair 3.25mm (US 3; UK 10) knitting needles

1 ball double knitting (8 ply) yarn

Small quantity of soft textured, high quality
safety stuffing

2 x 6mm round black beads for eyes

Black embroidery thread or floss for features

Sewing needles

Stitch holder

Instructions

Work entirely in GS, unless otherwise stated.

Head

Cast on 30 sts.

Rows 1–4: GS.

Row 5: K2, skpo, knit to last 3 sts, K2tog, K1.

Rows 6–7: GS.

Continue to dec in this way on every third row until
8 sts rem.

Next row: K2, skpo, K2tog, K2.

Next row: K2, skpo, K2.

Next row: K1, sl1, K2tog, psso, K1.

Next row: K3tog.

Fasten off.

Body and legs (make 2 pieces the same)

Cast on 12 sts.

Rows 1–2: GS.

Rows 3–8: inc 1 st at each end of rows 3, 5 and 7
[18 sts].

Rows 8–33: knit.

Row 34: divide for legs. K8, cast-off 2, knit to end
[8 sts].

Proceed on these 8 sts for first leg.

Rows 35–52: knit.

Row 53: K2tog, knit to last 2 sts, K2tog.

Row 54: cast off.

Return to stitches left on needle, rejoin yarn and
complete to match first leg.

Arms (make 2)

Cast on 6 sts.

Row 1: knit.

Row 2: knit twice into each st to end [12 sts].

Rows 3–6: knit.

Row 7: inc 1 st at each end of row [14 sts].

Rows 8–27: knit.

Rows 28–30: dec 1 st at each end of rows 28 and 30
[10 sts].

Row 31: K2, (K2tog) 3 times, K2 [7 sts].

Row 32: knit.

Cast off (this is the top of the arm).

Making up

1. Make up the head by folding the three corners of
the triangle into the centre; the fold lines are shown in
diagram 1 opposite. Sew the two side seams either
side of the nose, and across the corner lines to form the
ears, as shown in diagram 2.

2. Sew a little way along the neck seam, just down from the nose (diagram 3). Stuff the head firmly to give it a good shape. Stitch on the nose and mouth with black thread, and sew on the eyes.

3. Stitch the back and front body pieces together using a flat seam on the right side of the work. Leave the neck edge open for stuffing. Stuff firmly and then close the neck opening. Seam the arms and stuff, then attach the head to the body.

Actual size.

1

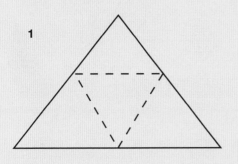

2

3

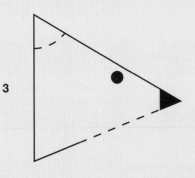

Stuffing

Be careful not to under- or over-stuff your bear otherwise its clothes may not fit properly. Check your bear's measurements as you go along to make sure it matches the one opposite.

Clothes

Shoes (make 2)

Using an appropriate colour and 3.25mm (US 3; UK 10) needles, cast on 14 sts.

Next row: knit.

Next row: inc in each st across row [28 sts].

Work 5 rows GS.

Next row: K2tog, K8, (K2tog) 4 times, K8, K2tog.

Next row: K9, (K2tog) twice, K9.

Next row: knit.

Cast off. Stitch the seam along the base and back of the shoe. Put a tiny amount of stuffing inside the shoe, place the base of the leg inside the shoe and stitch it in place. Add embellishments.

Trousers (make 2 pieces the same)

Using an appropriate colour and 3.25mm (US 3; UK 10) needles, cast on 13 sts.

Rows 1–4: GS.

Rows 5–20: SS, ending on a purl row. Break yarn and leave these 13 sts on a spare needle.

Now work another piece to match. Do not break off yarn but continue as follows:

Knit across 13 sts on needle, cast on 2 sts, work across 13 sts left on spare needle [28 sts].

Next row: purl.

*Work a further 2 rows in SS, ending on a purl row.

Next row: K2, skpo, knit to last 4 sts, K2tog, K2.

Next row: purl.*

Repeat from * to * [24 sts].

Work 4 rows in rib, or as given in instructions.

Dress

Bodice front

Cast on 24 sts.

Rows 1–6: SS.

Rows 7–8: cast off 2 sts at beg of each row.

Rows 9–10: SS.

Row 11: dec 1 st at each end of row [18 sts].

Row 12: purl.

Rows 13–16: SS.

Divide for neck

Work 7 sts, slip next 4 sts on to stitch holder for neck, turn and work 7 sts.

Continue on first 7 sts for side of neck.

Dec 1 st at neck edge on next and following alt rows until 4 sts rem.

Cast off.

Work other side to match.

Bodice back

Work rows 1–16 of bodice front.

Rows 17–21: SS.

Cast off.

Skirt

With RS facing, pick up and knit 24 sts along cast-on edge of bodice front.

Next row: purl.

Next row: knit twice into each st [48 sts].

Continue in SS and complete as given in pattern.

Repeat the above, on bodice back.

Neckband

Join one shoulder seam.

With RS facing, pick up and knit 5 sts down one side of neck, 4 sts from stitch holder across front of neck, 5 sts up other side of neck and 10 sts around back of neck (rem 4 sts will form other shoulder).

Next row: knit.

Cast off knitwise.

Katy Strawberry

Make the basic bear (see page 8).

Strawberry body

The two body parts are worked in strawberry pink yarn. Make two pieces the same, each beginning at the base, working in SS.

Cast on 8 sts, and work rows 1–2 SS.

Rows 3–7: continuing in SS, inc 1 st at each end of rows 3, 5 and 7 [14 sts].

Row 8: purl.

Rows 9–10: cast on 2 sts at beg of each row.

Rows 11–12: cast on 3 sts at beg of each row [24 sts].

Rows 13–15: inc 1 st at each end of rows 13 and 15 [28 sts].

Rows 16–21: SS, beg with a purl row.

Rows 22–28: dec 1 st at each end of rows 22, 24, 26 and 28 [20 sts].

Rows 29–30: SS, ending with a purl row.

Rows 31–32: cast off 2 sts at beg of each row.

Row 33: dec 1 st at each end of row.

Rows 34–36: SS.

Cast off.

Collar leaves (make 5)

Work all inc sts for the collar leaves by picking up the strand of yarn between the previous 2 sts and knitting into the back of it.

Using pale green, cast on 5 sts.

Row 1: purl.

Row 2: K2, inc, K1, inc, K2 [7 sts].

Row 3: knit.

Row 4: K3, inc, K1, inc, K3 [9 sts].

Row 5: knit.

Row 6: K4, inc, K1, inc, K4 [11 sts].

Row 7: knit.

Row 8: K5, inc, K1, inc, K5 [13 sts].

Rows 9–13: knit.

Row 14: K2tog, knit to last 2 sts, K2tog [11 sts].

Rows 15: knit.

Row 16: repeat row 14 [9 sts].

Row 17: knit.

Row 18: repeat row 14 [7 sts].

Row 19: K2tog, K3, K2tog [5 sts]

Row 20: K2tog, K1, K2tog [3 sts]

Row 21: P3tog. Fasten off.

Small leaf

Using pale green, cast on 3 sts.

Next row: K1, inc in next st, K1 [4 sts].

Work 4 rows GS.

Next row: dec 1 st at each end of row.

Next row: K2tog.

Fasten off.

Shoes

Follow basic shoes pattern (page 10), using pale green.

Making up

Stitch the body parts together at the base and sew up the side seams. Slip the body on to the bear and place small amounts of stuffing into the space between the bear and the body, shaping it as you go. Stitch the shoulder seams. Catch the body in places around the legs and the armholes, and along the neck edge. Sew on gold beads randomly to represent seeds. Sew the shoes on to the bear and stitch the small flower buttons on to the shoe fronts. Sew the large flower button and small leaf on to the bear's head. Sew the five larger leaves together in a circle to form the collar, and stitch in place around the bear's neck.

What you need

1 pair 3.25mm (US 3; UK 10) knitting needles

1 ball strawberry pink double knitting (8 ply)

1 ball pale green double knitting (8 ply)

Small amount of safety stuffing

1 large and 2 small flower buttons

Small gold beads for seeds on strawberry

Materials for basic bear, including light beige double knitting (8 ply)

Baby Oliver

Make the basic bear (see page 8). When making up the bear, sew across the tops of the legs where they join to the body, so that the legs bend.

Top (make 2 pieces the same, front and back)

Using blue yarn, cast on 24 sts.
Row 1: knit.
Work in pattern as follows:
Row 2: (WS facing) (K1, P1) to end of row.
Row 3: knit.
Rows 4–7: repeat rows 2 and 3, twice.
Rows 8–9: continuing in pattern, cast off 2 sts at beg of each row.
Rows 10–19: repeat rows 2 and 3, 5 times.
Rows 20–23: GS.
Cast off.

Nappy

Using white yarn, cast on 24 sts.
Rows 1–4: work in K1, P1 rib.
Rows 5–10: SS.
Continue in SS.

To shape legs:
Rows 11–12: cast off 4 sts at beg of each row.
Rows 13–14: cast off 3 sts at beg of each row.
Row 15: K2tog at each end of row [8 sts].

Row 16: purl.
Rows 17–18: repeat rows 15 and 16 [6 sts].
Rows 19–28: SS.
Rows 29–31: inc 1 st at each end of rows 29 and 31 [10 sts].
Row 32: purl.
Rows 33–34: cast on 3 sts at beg of each row.
Rows 35–36: cast on 4 sts at beg of each row [24 sts].
Rows 37–42: SS.
Rows 43–46: (K1, P1) rib to end of row.
Cast off in rib.

Bootees

Using blue yarn, follow instructions for basic shoes on page 10.

Making up

Work in the ends, sew the side seams of the nappy and slip the nappy on to the bear. Sew the side seams of the bear's top, slip it on to the bear and catch the shoulder seams together. Iron the motif on to the front of the top. Tie the comforter button on to a length of ribbon and hang it around the bear's neck. Sew up the seams of the bootees, tie tiny bows and attach them to the fronts. Sew the bootees on to the bear.

What you need

- 1 pair 3.25mm (US 3; UK 10) knitting needles
- 1 ball white double knitting (8 ply)
- 1 ball blue double knitting (8 ply)
- 20in (50cm) narrow, pale blue ribbon
- 1 comforter button
- Tiny iron-on teddy nursery motif
- Materials for basic bear, including light brown double knitting (8 ply)

Peter Pumpkin

Make the basic bear (see page 8).

Pumpkin body
Make 2 body pieces the same, starting at the base. Work in SS. Using orange, cast on 8 sts and work rows 1 and 2 in SS.
Rows 3–7: continuing in SS, inc 1 st at each end of rows 3, 5 and 7 [14 sts].
Row 8: purl.
Rows 9–10: cast on 2 sts at beg of each row.
Rows 11–12: cast on 3 sts at beg of each row [24 sts].
Rows 13–15: inc 1 st at each end of rows 13 and 15 [28 sts].
Rows 16–21: SS, beg with a purl row.
Rows 22–30: dec 1 st at each end of rows 22, 24, 26 and 30 [20 sts].
Rows 31–32: SS, ending with a purl row.
Rows 33–34: cast off 2 sts at beg of each row.
Row 35: dec 1 st at each end of row [14 sts].
Rows 36–38: SS (this is the neck edge).
Cast off.

Hat
Using orange, cast on 8 sts.
Row 1: purl.
Row 2: inc in each st to end of row [16 sts].
Row 3: purl.
Row 4: (K1, inc in next st) to end.
Row 5: purl.
Row 6: (K2, inc in next st) to end.
Rows 7–9: SS, beg with a purl row.
Cast off.

Pumpkin stalk
Using brown, cast on 6 sts.
Rows 1–5: GS.
Cast off.

Leaves (make 2)
Work all inc sts for the leaves by picking up the strand of yarn between the previous 2 sts and knitting into the back of it.
Using green, cast on 5 sts.
Row 1: purl.
Row 2: K2, inc, K1, inc, K2 [7 sts].
Row 3: knit.
Row 4: K3, inc, K1, inc, K3 [9 sts].
Rows 5–8: knit.
Dec 1 st at each end of every following alt row until 3 sts rem.
K3tog.
Fasten off.

Making up
Stitch the body parts together at the base, then join the side seams. Slip the body on to the bear and stuff lightly to give a rounded shape. Sew the shoulder seams, then secure the body to the bear by stitching all around the armholes and legs. Sew up the hat seam, stitch the stalk together lengthwise, and attach the stalk to the top of the hat. Stuff the hat lightly and sew it to the head. Cut out shapes for the eyes, nose and mouth from black felt (use the photograph as a guide). Stitch them in place. Stitch the leaves together and secure to the bear's shoulder.

What you need

1 pair 3.25mm (US 3; UK 10) knitting needles

1 ball green double knitting (8 ply)

1 ball orange double knitting (8 ply)

Oddments of brown double knitting (8 ply)

Black felt for pumpkin features

Small amount of safety stuffing

Materials for basic bear, including green double knitting (8 ply)

Freddy Footballer

Make the basic bear (see page 8). When working the legs, after 4 rows of yellow change to the stripe pattern of 2 rows red, 2 rows white for the socks.

Shirt

Back:

Using red, cast on 24 sts.

Rows 1–4: K2, P2 rib.

Rows 5–10: change to white and SS for 6 rows, beg with a knit row.

To shape armholes (raglan shaping):

Rows 11–12: cast off 2 sts at beg of each row.

Row 13: K1, skpo, knit to last 3 sts, K2tog, K1.

Row 14: purl.

Repeat rows 13–14 until 8 sts rem, ending on a purl row. Leave sts on a stitch holder.

Sleeves (make 2):

Using red, cast on 24 sts.

Rows 1–4: K2, P2 rib.

Rows 5–8: change to white and SS for 4 rows.

Shape top as for back.

Front:

Work as back until 14 sts rem after raglan shaping, then divide for neck.

Next row: K1, skpo, K2, turn and leave rem sts on a stitch holder.

Next row: purl.

Next row: K1, skpo, K1.

Next row: purl.

Next row: K3tog.

Fasten off.

Slip first 4 sts on to safety pin for centre neck, join yarn to remaining sts and complete to match first side, reversing shaping and working K2tog in place of skpo.

Neckband:

Using red, pick up and knit 8 sts across top of sleeve, then 5 sts down left side of neck, 4 sts across centre front, 5 sts up right side of neck, 8 sts across other sleeve and 8 sts across back.

GS for 3 rows.

Cast off firmly.

Shorts (make 2 pieces the same)

Using white, cast on 13 sts.

Rows 1–2: GS.

Rows 3–8: SS, beg with a knit row.

Break yarn and leave these 13 sts on a spare needle.

Work another piece to match, but this time do not break off yarn.

Continue as follows:

Row 9: knit across 13 sts on needle, cast on 2 sts, work across 13 sts left on spare needle [28 sts].

Row 10: purl.

Rows 11–12: SS, beg with a knit row.

Row 13: K1, skpo, knit to last 3 sts, K2tog, K1.

Row 14: purl.

Rows 15–18: repeat rows 11–14 [24 sts].

Rows 19–22: K2, P2 rib.

Cast off in rib.

Boots

Using black yarn, follow instructions for basic shoes on page 10. Once attached to the bear's legs, sew a few stitches using white yarn to represent laces.

Football

Using white yarn, make a ball following the instructions on pages 20–21.

What you need

1 pair 3.25mm (US 3; UK 10) knitting needles

1 ball white double knitting (8 ply)

1 ball red double knitting (8 ply)

Oddment of black double knitting (8 ply) for boots and embroidery

Small amount of safety stuffing

Materials for basic bear, including yellow double knitting (8 ply)

Making up

Sew the seams on the shorts and put them on to the bear. Sew the seams on the shirt, but leave the back raglan seam and neckband open. Slip the shirt on to the bear and join up the remaining seam. Using black, embroider a number on the back using chain stitch and a tiny badge on the front; use the photograph as a guide.

Toby the Toddler

Make the basic bear (see page 8).

Dungarees

Front:

Using denim blue, cast on 13 sts.

Rows 1–4: GS.

Rows 5–20: SS, ending on a purl row. Break yarn and leave these 13 sts on a spare needle.

Now work another piece to match. Do not break off yarn but continue as follows:

Row 21: knit across 13 sts on needle, cast on 2 sts, work across 13 sts left on spare needle [28 sts].

Row 22: purl.

Rows 23–24: SS, ending on a purl row.

Row 25: K2, skpo, knit to last 4 sts, K2tog, K2.

Row 26: purl.

Rows 27–30: repeat rows 23–26 [24 sts].

Rows 31–34: GS.

Bib:

Row 35: (RS facing) cast off 8 sts (1 st left on needle), knit a further 7 sts, cast off rem 8 sts.

Turn and continue to work on rem 8 sts.

Row 36: (WS facing) K2, P4, K2.

Row 37: knit.

Rows 38–41: repeat rows 36–37 twice.

Row 42: as row 36.

Rows 43–46: GS.

Row 47: K2, cast off 4 sts, K2.

Working on first set of 2 sts for straps, continue in GS until strap fits over shoulder and down to waist on back of bear. Cast off.

Return to other set of 2 sts and make a second strap to match. Cast off.

Back:

Work as front of dungarees (rows 1–34).

Cast off.

Patch:

Using a colour of your choice, cast on 6 sts.

Work 10 rows in GS.

Cast off.

Ball

Using turquoise, cast on 6 sts.

Row 1: purl.

Row 2: inc in each st across row [12 sts].

Row 3: purl.

Row 4: (K1, inc in next st) across row [18 sts].

Row 5: purl.

Row 6: (K2, inc in next st) across row [24 sts].

Row 7: purl.

Rows 8–9: SS.

Break yarn.

Change to orange yarn.

Rows 10–13: GS, beg with a knit row.

Break yarn and join in green yarn.

Rows 14–15: SS, ending with purl row.

Row 16: (K2, K2tog) across row [18 sts].

Row 17: purl.

Row 18: (K1, K2tog) across row [12 sts].

Row 19: purl.

Row 20: K2tog across row [6 sts].

Row 21: purl.

Break yarn and run end through rem sts. Pull up tight and secure.

What you need

- 1 pair 3.25mm (US 3; UK 10) knitting needles
- 1 ball denim blue double knitting (8 ply)
- Oddments of turquoise, green and orange yarn
- Black embroidery thread
- Small candy cane button
- Small amount of safety stuffing
- Materials for basic bear, including beige double knitting (8 ply)

Making up
Sew the seams of the dungarees, slip them on to the bear, cross the straps behind the bear's head and secure them on the back waistband. Place the patch on the dungaree knee (as shown in the photograph) and stitch it in place using large stitches. For the ball, Sew the side seam, and stuff the ball to give a rounded shape before closing. Sew the candy cane button inside the waistband.

Billy Bridegroom

Make the basic bear (see page 8).

Waistcoat

Front (make 2 pieces the same and work in moss stitch):
Using grey, cast on 3 sts.
Row 1: K1, P1, K1.
Row 2: inc in next st, P1, inc in next st.
Row 3: P1, K1, P1, K1, P1.
Row 4: inc in next st, K1, P1, K1, inc in next st.
Row 5: (K1, P1) 3 times, K1.
Row 6: (K1, P1) 3 times, K1.
Row 7: (K1, P1) 3 times, K1.
Row 8: inc, (P1, K1) 2 times, inc.
Row 9: (P1, K1) 4 times, P1.
Row 10: (P1, K1) 4 times, P1.
Row 11: inc, (K1, P1) 3 times, K1, inc.
Row 12: (K1, P1) 5 times, K1.
Row 13: inc, (P1, K1) 4 times, P1, inc.
Row 14: (P1, K1) 6 times, P1 [13 sts].
Rows 15–16: continue in pattern.
Row 17: K2tog, pattern to end.
Row 18: cast off 2 sts, pattern to end.
Row 19: P2tog, pattern to last 2 sts, K2tog [8 sts].
Rows 20–26: dec 1 st at beg of row and at this edge on every alt row until 4 sts rem.
Rows 27–28: work in pattern.
Cast off.

Back:
Cast on 24 sts.
Rows 1–2: knit.
Rows 3–8: SS.
Shape arms and complete as for basic dress – bodice back (page 11).

Trousers

Using black yarn, follow instructions for basic trousers (page 10).

Cravat

Using white, cast on 16 sts.
Rows 1–20: SS, ending with a purl row.
Row 21: dec 1 st at each end of row.
Row 22: purl.
Repeat rows 21–22 until 10 sts remain.
Work 6 rows SS. Cast off.

Making up

Sew the shoulder seams of the waistcoat, then sew the side seams. Sew the wide edge of the cravat to the centre neck of the bear under his chin. Pouch it slightly then stitch the pearl bead on to the cravat to represent a tie pin. Put on the waistcoat and secure it with the two gold beads. Refer to the photograph as a guide. Sew the trouser seams and put the trousers on to the bear. Tuck the end of the cravat into the top of the trousers. Secure the white paper rose as a buttonhole in the waistcoat.

What you need

1 pair 3.25mm (US 3; UK 10) knitting needles

1 ball black double knitting (8 ply)

1 ball grey double knitting (8 ply)

Oddment of sparkly white double knitting (8 ply) for cravat

2 small gold beads for buttons

1 small, white paper rose

1 pearl bead

Materials for basic bear, including beige double knitting (8 ply)

Grace Bride

Make the basic bear (see page 8).

Dress

Using sparkly white yarn, follow instructions for basic dress on page 11, but when working the skirt continue until work measures 2¾in (7cm). Work 4 rows in moss stitch. Cast off.

Making up the dress

Stitch one shoulder seam and work the neckband in moss stitch. Sew the side seams, turn right-side out and slip the dress on to the bear. Catch together the neckband and the shoulder seam neatly. Tie the ribbon around the bear's waist and finish with a bow at the back.

Headdress and veil

Gather a short length of narrow satin ribbon into a circle, a little bigger than the pearl and rose embellishment, and secure it to the roses with a few stitches. Fold the net into an oblong and gather it at the top to give it a nice shape. Stitch it to the headdress.

Bouquet

Gather the lace edging into a circle. Slip the bunch of roses through the centre and secure. Sew each side of the bouquet to the bear's paws to hold it in place.

Necklace

Thread the pearl beads on to a piece of strong thread and make a string of them long enough to go around the bear's neck. Knot and secure. Tie the necklace around the bear's neck.

What you need

1 pair 3.25mm (US 3; UK 10) knitting needles

1 ball sparkly white double knitting (8 ply)

Small piece of net for veil

Short length of narrow satin ribbon, pearl and rose embellishment for headdress

10in (25cm) narrow lace edging

6 white paper roses for bouquet

30 small pearl beads for necklace

Strong thread for sewing and for threading beads

40in (1m) white satin ribbon, ¼in (5mm) wide

Materials for basic bear, including pale beige double knitting (8 ply)

Pippa Dolly

Make the basic bear (see page 8).

Dress

Back:

Using deep mauve, cast on 44 sts.
Rows 1–3: GS.
Change to lilac.
Rows 1–4 form the pattern.
Row 1: (RS facing) knit.
Row 2: purl.
Row 3: K2, *yrn, P1, P3tog, P1, yon, K2*, rep from * to * to end.
Row 4: purl.
Rows 5–16: repeat rows 1–4, 3 times.
Row 17: K2tog across row [22 sts].
Row 18: knit.
Row 19: K2, (yfwd, K2tog, K1) to last 2 sts, yfwd, K2tog.
Row 20: knit.
Rows 21–24: SS.
Row 25: cast off 2 sts, knit to end.
Row 26: cast off 2 sts, purl to end.
Row 27: K1, skpo, knit to last 3 sts, K2tog, K1.
Row 28: purl.
Repeat rows 27 and 28 until 6 sts rem, ending on a purl row. Slip sts on to a stitch holder.

Sleeves (make two the same):

Using deep mauve, cast on 22 sts.
Rows 1–3: GS.
Change to lilac.
Rows 4–8: SS, ending with a purl row.
Continue from row 25 of the dress back (see page 11), ending with 6 sts. Slip sts on to a stitch holder.

Front:

Follow instructions for back to row 28.
Continue shaping until 12 sts remain, ending with a purl row.

To shape neck:

Next row: K2, K2tog, turn. Leave rem sts on a stitch holder.
Next row: purl.
Next row: K1, K2tog, turn.
Next row: purl.
Next row: K2tog, fasten off.
Return to sts on holder. Slip next 4 sts on to a safety pin for front of neck.

Shape other side of neck:

Next row: K2tog, K2.
Next row: purl.
Next row: K2tog, K1.
Next row: purl.
Next row: K2tog.
Fasten off.

Neckband:

Using deep mauve, pick up and knit 31 sts all around neck.
Work 3 rows GS. Cast off.

Shoes

Using deep mauve yarn, follow instructions for basic shoes on page 10.

Making up

Sew the seams of the dress, but leave the left back raglan and neckband open. Slip the dress on to the bear and join the remaining seams. Thread the ribbon through the holes at the waist and tie in a bow. Sew the shoes on to the bear (see page 10) and attach the button on the fronts. Attach the doll to the bear's paw with a few stitches and sew the paw to the body to hold it in place. Sew the tiny bow to the bear's head.

What you need

- 1 pair 3.25mm (US 3; UK 10) knitting needles
- 1 ball deep mauve double knitting (8 ply)
- 1 ball lilac double knitting (8 ply)
- 10in (25cm) narrow ribbon in deep mauve
- Tiny doll
- 2 small buttons
- Tiny mauve bow embellishment
- Materials for basic bear, including white double knitting (8 ply)

Christmas Holly

Make the basic bear (see page 8).

Dress

Follow instructions for basic dress (see page 11), using red yarn.
When skirt measures 2¼in (6cm), change to white.
Work 3 rows GS.
Cast off.
Work the neckband using white.

Sleeves (make 2 the same):
Using white, cast on 24 sts.
Rows 1–2: knit.
Break yarn and join in red.
Rows 3–10: SS.
Cast off.

Boots

Using red yarn, follow instructions for basic shoes on page 10.
For tops of boots, cast on 16 sts in white and knit 2 rows. Cast off.

Muff

Using white, cast on 18 sts.
Rows 1–2: GS.
Join in red yarn.
Rows 3–12: SS, ending with a purl row.
Rows 13–14: GS, using white yarn.
Cast off.

Hat

Using white, cast on 36 sts.
Rows 1–10: GS.
Break white yarn and join in red.
Rows 11–16: SS.

To shape top of hat:
Row 17: (K4, skpo) across row [30 sts].
Rows 18–20: SS.
Row 21: (K3, skpo) across row [24 sts].
Row 22: purl.
Row 23: (K2, skpo) across row [18 sts].
Row 24: purl.
Row 25: K2tog across row [9 sts].
Break yarn and thread through rem sts. Pull tight and fasten off.

Making up

Sew the side seams of the dress and turn right-side out. Slip the dress on to the bear. Catch together the neckband and shoulder seam neatly. Sew the sleeve seams then stitch the sleeves to the armholes. Attach the boots to the bear's legs (see page 10). Stitch the white tops around the tops of the boots, attaching each one to the boot and to the bear's leg. Sew on the star buttons. Stitch the side seam of the muff, roll it into a cylinder shape and attach the star button to the front. Cut a length of ribbon long enough to form a strap and stitch it inside the muff, making sure the ribbon join is hidden inside. Join the side seam of the hat and turn back the brim. Make a tiny pom-pom and sew it to the top of the hat. Place the hat on the bear's head and secure. Sew the candle button on the front.

What you need

- 1 pair 3.25mm (US 3; UK 10) knitting needles
- 1 ball red double knitting (8 ply)
- 1 ball sparkly white double knitting (8 ply)
- 3 gold star buttons
- 1 candle button
- 40in (1m) red satin ribbon, ¼in (5mm) wide
- Materials for basic bear, including light beige double knitting (8 ply)

Abi Ballerina

Make the basic bear (see page 8).

Dress

Using pink yarn, follow instructions for basic dress (see page 11). When skirt measures 2in (5cm), work 2 rows GS. Cast off.

Making up the dress:

Stitch one shoulder seam and work the neckband. Sew the side seams, turn right-side out and slip the dress on to the bear. Catch together the neckband and shoulder seam. Tie a length of ribbon around the waist and tie in a bow at the back. Attach the ribbon, pearl and rose embellishment to the front of the dress at the waistline. Stitch the pink edging around the hem and neckline.

Ballet slippers

Using pink yarn, follow instructions for basic shoes on page 10, but work in SS. Attach the slippers to the bear's legs following the basic instructions. Take a short length of pink ribbon, approximately 3¼in (8cm) long, and stitch one end to the right-hand side of the left-hand slipper at the front. Take it across the front of the shoe to the left, and wrap it around the back of the bear's leg. Bring it back round to the front and catch it in place on the left-hand side of the slipper. Sew a ribbon rose to the centre front. Finish the other slipper to match.

Finishing off

Take the net and fold it in half lengthwise. Gather the folded edge (this is the top) until it fits around the bear's waist. Slip it on to the bear and secure. Sew the side seam. Catch it in place under the skirt of the dress. Make a small bow with pink ribbon and stitch two ribbon roses to the centre of it. Place the decoration on the bear's head and stitch it in place. Use the photograph as a guide.

What you need

- 1 pair 3.25mm (US 3; UK 10) knitting needles
- 1 ball pale pink double knitting (8 ply)
- Pink net for under skirt, 4 x 15¾in (10 x 40cm)
- 1 pink satin ribbon, pearl and rose embellishment
- 4 small ribbon roses
- 20in (50cm) sparkly pink ribbon edging
- Strong thread for sewing
- 40in (1m) pink double-sided satin ribbon, ¼in (5mm) wide
- Materials for basic bear, including light beige double knitting (8 ply)

What you need

1 pair 3.25mm (US 3; UK 10) knitting needles

1 ball cream double knitting (8 ply)

1 ball deep turquoise double knitting (8 ply)

Materials for basic bear, including grey double knitting (8 ply)

Barney Bear

Make the basic bear (see page 8).

Sweatshirt

Front:
Using cream, cast on 26 sts.
Rows 1–3: moss stitch.
Rows 4–5: SS.
Now place the motif, using the chart for guidance:
Row 6: K10, join in turquoise and K7, change back to cream and K9. This forms the base of the 'B'.
Rows 7–15: continue working from the chart until the motif is complete.
Rows 16–18: SS.
Rows 19–21: moss stitch.
Cast off.

Back:
Work as front, but omit the motif.

Sleeves (make 2 the same):
Using cream, cast on 25 sts.
Rows 1–3: moss stitch.
Rows 4–5: SS.
Rows 6–7: join in turquoise, and SS.
Rows 8–9: SS using cream.
Rows 10–11: SS using turquoise.
Rows 12–13: SS using cream.
Cast off. (This is the top of the sleeve.)

Pants

Using turquoise yarn, follow instructions for basic trousers (page 10).

Side stripe:
Using cream, cast on 20 sts.
Knit 1 row.
Cast off.

Making up

Work in the yarn ends on the sweatshirt, and stitch the shoulder seams for 5 sts in from each side. Fold the sleeves in half lengthways and mark the centre point at the top. Stitch them in place along the sides of the sweatshirt, matching the centre point to the shoulder seam. Now join the side and sleeve seams. Slip the sweatshirt over the bear's head. Join the trouser seams, stitch the stripe on to the side seam and put the trousers on to the bear.

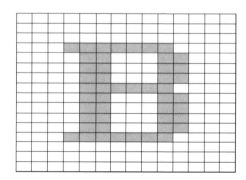

Sweet Honey Bee

Make the basic bear (see page 8) using black for the body, legs and arms and yellow for the head.

Bee body

The two body parts are worked in black and yellow yarn. Make two pieces the same, each beginning at the base, working in SS. Start with 6 rows yellow, then 4 rows black. Repeat until the third black stripe is completed, then continue in yellow only.

Using yellow, cast on 8 sts.
Rows 1–2: SS.
Rows 3–7: continuing in SS, inc 1 st at each end of rows 3, 5 and 7 [14 sts].
Row 8: purl.
Rows 9–10: cast on 2 sts at beg of each row.
Rows 11–12: cast on 3 sts at beg of each row [24 sts].
Rows 13–15: inc 1 st at each end of rows 13 and 15 [28 sts].
Rows 16–21: SS, beg with a purl row.
Rows 22–28: dec 1 st at each end of rows 22, 24, 26 and 28 [20 sts].
Rows 29–30: SS, ending with a purl row.
Rows 31–32: cast off 2 sts at beg of each row.
Row 33: dec 1 st at each end of row [14 sts].
Rows 34–36: SS.
Cast off.

Wings

Large (make 2):
Using cream, cast on 8 sts.
Rows 1–2: knit.
Rows 3–9: inc 1 st at each end of rows 3, 5, 7 and 9 [16 sts].
Rows 10–17: GS.
Rows 18–28: dec 1 st at each end of rows 18, 20, 22, 24, 26 and 28 [4 sts].
Cast off.

Small (make 2):
Using cream, cast on 6 sts.
Rows 1–2: knit.
Rows 3–9: inc 1 st at each end of rows 3, 5, 7 and 9 [14 sts].
Rows 10–15: GS.
Dec 1 st at each end of next and every alt row until 4 sts remain.
Cast off.

Making up

Sew the base and side seams of the body pieces, matching the stripes. Slip the body on to the bear, stuff lightly to give a rounded shape, and sew the shoulder seams. Now catch the body pieces to the bear around the legs, arms and neck edge to secure. Sew the wings together in pairs, with the small wing on top of the large wing, and secure them to the bear at the back of the neck. Make the antennae using a piece of black yarn. Thread it through the top of the head. Roll each end into a tight circle and stitch to secure. Thread the flower stems through the paw and secure the paw to the body.

What you need

1 pair 3.25mm (US 3; UK 10) knitting needles
1 ball black double knitting (8 ply)
1 ball yellow double knitting (8 ply)
1 ball cream double knitting (8 ply)
Small amount of safety stuffing
2 small silk flowers and a leaf
Materials for basic bear, including yellow and black double knitting (8 ply)

Olivia Sweetheart

Make the basic bear (see page 8).

Trousers

Follow instructions for basic trousers (see page 10). Work the first 4 rows of the trouser legs in moss stitch using pink, and the remainder of the trousers in SS stripes of 2 rows cream and 2 rows pink. The waistband is worked in moss stitch.

Sweater

Back:

Using cream, cast on 25 sts.
Rows 1–4: moss stitch.
Rows: 5–10: SS.

To shape armholes:
Rows 11–12: continue in SS, and cast off 2 sts at beg of each row.
Row 13: K1, skpo, knit to last 3 sts, K2tog, K1.
Row 14: purl.
Repeat rows 13 and 14 until 9 sts remain, ending with a purl row. Leave sts on a stitch holder.

Sleeves (make 2 the same):
Using cream, cast on 25 sts.
Rows 1–4: moss stitch.
Rows 5–8: SS.
Shape top as for back.

Front:

Using cream, cast on 25 sts.
Rows 1–4: moss stitch.
Rows 5–8: SS.
Now place the heart motif, working from the chart.
Row 9: K12, join in pink and K1, change back to cream and K12.
Rows 10–17: continue to follow chart, and shape armholes as for back.
When 15 sts rem, divide for neck:
Row 18: K1, skpo, K2, turn and leave rem sts on a stitch holder.
Row 19: purl.
Row 20: K1, skpo, K1.
Row 21: purl.
Row 22: K3tog.
Fasten off.
Slip first 5 sts on to safety pin for centre neck, join yarn to remaining sts and complete to match back, reversing the shaping and working K2tog in place of skpo.

Neckband:

Using cream, work in moss stitch. Pick up and knit sts across top of one sleeve, 5 sts on left side of front, 5 sts across centre neck, 5 sts on right side of front, sts from other sleeve, and finally sts from back.
Moss stitch for 3 rows.
Cast off.

Making up

Sew up the trousers, matching the stripes. Sew up the sweater and slip it over the bear's head before joining the final raglan seam and neckband. Complete the sewing up. Make a small pink bow and stitch it on to the bear's head.

What you need

1 pair 3.25mm (US 3; UK 10) knitting needles

1 ball cream double knitting (8 ply)

1 ball pink double knitting (8 ply)

Small piece of narrow pink ribbon

Materials for basic bear, including pale pink double knitting (8 ply)

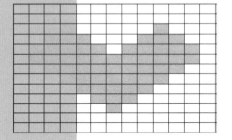

Knitting Emily

Make the basic bear (see page 8).

Dress

Back and front (both worked the same):
Using pale green, cast on 24 sts.
Rows 1–4: SS.
Rows 5–6: cast off 2 sts at beg of each row [20 sts].
Rows 7–8: SS.
Row 9: K2tog, knit to last 2 sts, K2tog.
Row 10: purl.
Rows 11–16: SS.
Rows 17–18: change to white and GS.
Cast off.
Using pale green, work skirt as for basic dress.
When work measures 2¾in (7cm) change to white and work 2 rows GS.
Cast off.

Apron

Using cream, cast on 36 sts.
Rows 1–4: GS.
Row 5: knit.
Row 6: K3, purl to last 3 sts, K3.
Rows 7–16: repeat rows 5 and 6, 5 times.
Row 17: (K3, K2tog) to last 3 sts, K3 [21 sts].
Row 18: cast on 18 sts, knit to end.
Row 19: cast on 18 sts, knit to end.
Row 20: knit across all sts.
Cast off.
Work in all the yarn ends. Embroider a small flower and leaf on to one corner of the apron using pink and green.

Slippers

Using pale green, cast on 14 sts.
Row 1: knit.
Row 2: inc in each st to end [28 sts]. Continue in GS.
Rows 3–4: knit using green.
Rows 5–6: knit using pink.
Row 7: knit using green.
Complete the slippers following instructions for basic shoes on page 10, from first dec row.

Glasses

Take a short length of fuse wire and twist it around a pencil to give two small circles. Arrange them into a pleasing shape, making sure they fit over the bear's eyes. Use the photograph for guidance. Bend each end of the wire to form the arms and push them into the bear's head on each side of the eyes. Secure with a few stitches.

Knitting

Cast on 10 sts and work 18 rows GS. Do not cast off.

Making up

Lightly stuff the slippers and sew them to the bear's legs (see page 10). Sew a cotton ball to the front of each slipper. Sew the side seams on the dress, slip it on to the bear and sew the shoulder seams. Sew the two heart buttons on the front. Tie the apron around the bear's waist and secure the ties with a few stitches. Make knitting needles by breaking a cocktail stick in half and gluing a bead on to the broken end of each one. Slip the knitting on to both tiny needles, and secure the needles on to the bear's paws with a dab of glue.

What you need

- 1 pair 3.25mm (US 3; UK 10) knitting needles
- 1 ball pale green double knitting (8 ply)
- 1 ball white double knitting (8 ply)
- Oddments of green, pink and yellow yarn
- 2 tiny pearl, heart-shaped buttons
- Cocktail stick
- 2 small cotton balls for slippers
- Fuse wire for glasses
- 2 small white beads for ends of knitting needles
- All-purpose glue
- Materials for basic bear, including light brown double knitting (8 ply)

Bikini Bear

Make the basic bear (see page 8).

Bikini

Top:

Using pink, cast on 40 sts.

Rows 1–4: GS.

Rows 5–6: cast off 12 sts, knit to end [16 sts].

Row 7: K8, turn and continue on this set of sts.

Rows 8–10: K2tog at end of each row [2 sts].

Row 11: K2tog [1 st].

Row 12: K1, turn.

Repeat row 12 until work measures 4in (10cm). Fasten off.

Rejoin yarn to rem 8 sts and complete to match the first side.

Pants:

Using pink, cast on 24 sts.

Rows 1–4: GS.

Rows 5–6: cast off 4 sts at beg of each row.

Rows 7–8: cast off 3 sts at beg of each row.

Row 9: knit.

Row 10: K2tog at each end of row [8 sts].

Rows 11–12: repeat rows 9–10 [6 sts].

Rows 13–20: GS.

Rows 21–23: inc 1 st at each end of rows 21 and 23 [10 sts].

Row 24: knit.

Rows 25–26: cast on 3 sts at beg of each row.

Rows 27–28: cast on 4 sts at beg of each row [24 sts].

Rows 29–32: GS.

Cast off.

Beach bag

Using pale pink, cast on 12 sts.

Rows 1–2: GS.

Change to SS and work *2 rows blue, 2 rows green, 2 rows pink*. Repeat from * to * until a total of 13 stripes have been worked, ending on a blue stripe. Using pink, work 2 rows in GS.

Cast off.

Handle:

Cast on 24 sts using pale pink yarn. Cast off.

Making up

Stitch the side seams of the bikini pants. Stitch rickrack braid around the waist. Slip the pants on to the bear and catch them in place with a few stitches. Stitch braid along the bottom edge of the bikini top. Place the top on the bear and stitch it in place. Tie it around the back of the neck to secure, using the photograph as a guide. Stitch the side seams of the bag, sew on the handle and attach the flower and leaf button. Stitch the sunglasses to the paw. Sew the tiny gold bead on to the front of the bear for a belly button stud.

What you need

1 pair 3.25mm (US 3; UK 10) knitting needles

1 ball pink double knitting (8 ply)

Oddments of pale pink, green, blue yarn

10in (25cm) lilac rickrack braid

Sunglasses embellishment

Flower and leaf button

Tiny gold bead

Materials for basic bear, including dark brown double knitting (8 ply)

Poppy Panda

Make the basic bear (see page 8), but do not attach the eyes. Knit the head using white yarn, and the arms using black. When working the body, begin with black yarn, continue until all shaping is complete, then change to white yarn. Continue with white until you divide for the legs, then change to black yarn. Complete the legs using black. Make both sides to match.

Eye patches (make 2)

Using black yarn, cast on 3 sts.
Row 1: knit.
Row 2: inc 1 st at each end of row.
Rows 3–6: GS.
Row 7: dec 1 st at each end of row.
Row 8: knit.
Row 9: sl1, k2tog, psso.
Fasten off.

Ears (make 2)

Using black yarn, cast on 3 sts.
Row 1: knit.
Row 2: inc 1 st at each end of row.
Rows 3–8: GS.
Row 9: dec 1 st at each end of row.
Row 10: knit.
Row 11: sl1, k2tog, psso.
Fasten off.

Making up

Position the eye patches either side of the bear's nose, using the photograph as a guide, and stitch them in place. Sew the eyes on top of the patches. Fold the ears in half, and place them over the ears that form part of the bear's head. Gather them slightly into shape and secure. Tie a piece of red ribbon around the bear's neck.

What you need

1 pair 3.25mm (US 3; UK 10) knitting needles

Oddments of black double knitting (8 ply) for eye patches and ears

10in (25cm) narrow red satin ribbon

Materials for basic bear, including black and white double knitting (8 ply)

Hiking Hector

Make the basic bear (see page 8). Knit the last few rows at the bottom of each leg using light blue yarn for socks.

Sweater

Back:
Using cream, cast on 24 sts.
Rows 1–4: K2, P2 rib.
Row 5: K9, P2, tw2, P2. K9.
Row 6: P9, K2, P2, K2, P9.
Rows 7–12: continue in pattern (rows 5 and 6).
To shape armholes, continue in pattern:
Rows 13–14: cast off 2 sts at each end of row.
Row 15: K1, skpo, pattern to last 3 sts, K2tog, K1.
Row 16: purl.
Repeat rows 15 and 16 until 8 sts rem, ending with a purl row. Leave the sts on a stitch holder.

Sleeves (make 2):
Using cream, cast on 24 sts.
Rows 1–4: K2, P2 rib.
Rows 5–8: SS.
Shape the top as for back, row 13 to end.

Front:
Work as for back until 14 sts rem after start of armhole shaping. Divide for neck.
K1, skpo, K2, turn and leave rem sts on a stitch holder.
Next row: purl.
Next row: K1, skpo, K1.
Next row: purl.
Next row: sl1, K2tog, psso.
Fasten off.
Slip centre 4 sts on to a holder and work on rem 5 sts for other side. Complete to match, reversing

shapings and working K2tog in place of skpo.

Neckband:
With RS facing, pick up and knit 8 sts across top of sleeve, 5 sts along left side of neck, 4 sts across neck front, 5 sts along right side of neck, 8 sts across top of second sleeve and 8 sts across neck back.
Work 5 rows SS, beg with a purl row. Cast off loosely.

Trousers

Follow instructions for basic trousers (page 10) using denim blue.

Making up the clothes

Stitch the raglan seams of the sweater, leaving the back left seam open. Stitch the side and sleeve seams. Put the sweater on to the bear and stitch the final seam and neckband. Sew up the trousers and put them on to the bear.

Boots

Using black yarn, follow instructions for basic shoes on page 10. Once attached to the bear's legs, sew a few stitches using red yarn to represent laces.

Backpack

Using royal blue, cast on 14 sts.
Row 1: knit.
Row 2: K2, purl to last 2 sts, K2.
Repeat rows 1 and 2 until work measures 4¾in (12cm).
Knit 2 rows GS, cast off.

Straps:
Using black, cast on 3 sts.
Work in moss stitch for 7in (18cm).
Cast off.

What you need

1 pair 3.25mm (US 3; UK 10) knitting needles

1 ball denim blue double knitting (8 ply)

1 ball cream double knitting (8 ply)

Oddments of red, black and royal blue double knitting (8 ply) for backpack and boots

Small amount of safety stuffing

Materials for basic bear, including beige and light blue double knitting (8 ply)

Making up the backpack
Fold the backpack into thirds, and join the side seams leaving the top third open for the flap. Stuff the backpack lightly, fold over the flap, and secure with two French knots. Sew the centre of the strap to the middle of the backpack at the back; catch the ends to each side at the base of the backpack to form loops.

Lucky Ladybird

Make the basic bear (see page 8) using black for the body, legs and arms and cream for the head.

Wings (make 2)

Work all inc sts for the wings by picking up the strand of yarn between the previous 2 sts and knitting into the back of it.

Using red, cast on 5 sts.

Row 1: purl.
Row 2: K2, inc, K1, inc, K2 [7 sts].
Row 3: knit.
Row 4: K3, inc, K1, inc, K3 [9 sts].
Row 5: knit.
Row 6: K4, inc, K1, inc, K4 [11 sts].
Row 7: knit.
Row 8: K5, inc, K1, inc, K5 [13 sts].
Continue to inc in this manner until 25 sts are on the needle.
Work 8 rows GS.
Dec 1 st at each end of each alt row until 7 sts rem.
Cast off.

Spots (make 6):
Using black, cast on 3 sts. Work in GS.
Row 1: knit.
Row 2: inc 1 st at each end of row.
Rows 3–6: GS.
Row 7: dec 1 st at each end of row.
Row 8: knit.
Row 9: sl1, K2tog, psso.
Fasten off.

Making up

Stitch three spots on each wing. Attach the wings to the bear, overlapping them slightly at the back neck. Tie the ribbon around the ladybird bear's neck. Make the antennae by threading a piece of black yarn through the top of the head and roll each end into a tight circle. Secure them with a few stitches. Sew the buttons on to the front of the bear.

What you need

- 1 pair 3.25mm (US 3; UK 10) knitting needles
- 1 ball red double knitting (8 ply)
- Oddments of black yarn for spots and antennae
- 3 ladybird buttons
- 20in (50cm) narrow red satin ribbon
- Materials for basic bear, including black and white double knitting (8 ply)

Pretty Party Bear

Make the basic bear (see page 8), working the last 5 rows of each leg in turquoise to represent socks.

Dress

Work 2 pieces the same, front and back (working from neck edge):
Using cream, cast on 18 sts.
Rows 1–8: K1, P1 rib.
Row 9: (K1, inc in next st) to end of row [27 sts].
Row 10: purl.
Row 11: K2, (yfwd, K2tog, K1) to last st, K1.
Row 12: purl.
Rows 13–14: SS, ending with a purl row.
Row 15: join in turquoise. K1 cream, K1 turquoise, (K3 cream, K1 turquoise) across row to last st, K1 cream. Break turquoise yarn.
Row 16: purl.
Row 17: inc 1 st at each end of row [29 sts].
Row 18: purl.
Rows 19–20: SS.
Row 21: inc 1 st at each end of row [31 sts].
Row 22: purl.
Row 23–25: repeat rows 15–17 [33 sts].
Rows 26–30: SS, ending with a purl row.
Rows 31–32: Join in turquoise and knit 2 rows.
Cast off in GS.

Shoulder straps (make 2):
Using cream, cast on 3 sts.
Row 1: K1, P1, K1.
Repeat row 1 until work measures 1½in (4cm). Cast off.

Handbag

Using cream, cast on 10 sts.
Row 1: K2, P6, K2.
Row 2: (RS facing) knit.
Repeat rows 1 and 2 until work measures 1½in (4cm).

To shape flap of bag:
Row 1: K2, skpo, K2, K2tog, K2.
Row 2: K2, P4, K2.
Row 3: K2, skpo, K2tog, K2.
Row 4: K2, P2, K2.
Row 5: K2, K2tog, K2.
Row 6: K2, P1, K2.
Row 7: K1, sl1, K2tog, psso, K1.
Row 8: K3.
Row 9: K3tog. Fasten off.

Handle:
Using turquoise, cast on 2 sts.
Row 1: K1, P1.
Row 2: P1, K1.
Repeat rows 1 and 2 until work measures 1½in (4cm). Cast off.

Making up

Sew the side seams of the dress up to the start of the ribbing. Match the patterns and the GS hem. Stitch one end of each shoulder strap on to the top of the dress. Slip the dress on to the bear. Pass the straps over the bear's shoulders and stitch them to the other side of the dress. Secure, and stitch a heart bead on to the ends of the straps at the front. Thread ribbon through the holes at the waist and tie in a bow. Make another tiny bow and sew it to the bear's head. Fold the piece of knitting for the handbag into thirds to make an envelope shape. Stitch the side seams. Attach a heart bead to the point of the flap. Thread the handle under the flap and secure.

What you need

1 pair 3.25mm (US 3; UK 10) knitting needles

1 ball cream double knitting (8 ply)

1 ball turquoise double knitting (8 ply)

6 heart-shaped turquoise glass beads

20in (50cm) narrow, fine ribbon with turquoise edging

Small amount of safety stuffing

Materials for basic bear, including brown double knitting (8 ply)

Shoes
Using cream yarn, follow instructions for basic shoes on page 10. When you have attached them to the bear, sew a heart button on the front of each one.

Ellie Bouquet

Make the basic bear (see page 8).

Dress

Using pale blue yarn, follow instructions for basic dress (see page 11).

When skirt measures 1½in (4cm), change to deep turquoise and work a further 4 rows SS, followed by 3 rows GS.

Cast off.

Sleeve frills (make 2):

Using pale blue, cast on 24 sts loosely.

Row 1: purl.

Row 2: knit, inc 12 sts evenly across row [36 sts].

Rows 3–4: SS.

Row 5: change to deep turquoise and knit 1 row.

Cast off.

Shoes

Using turquoise yarn, follow instructions for basic shoes on page 10. When you have attached them to the bear, sew a sparkly button on the front of each one.

Making up

Stitch one shoulder seam and work the neckband in deep turquoise. Sew the side seams, and turn right-side out. Slip the dress on to the bear. Catch together the neckband and shoulder seam neatly. Sew the sleeve frill ends together then stitch them to the armholes, easing to fit if needed. Tie a length of ribbon around the waist and finish with a bow at the back of the dress. Wrap some green yarn tightly around the base of the flowers, and secure. Catch the bear's paws to each side of the flowers to hold them in place. Tie a small bow from some ribbon and sew it to the top of the bear's head.

What you need

1 pair 3.25mm (US 3; UK 10) knitting needles

1 ball pale blue double knitting (8 ply)

Oddment of deep turquoise and green yarn

20in (50cm) deep turquoise narrow velvet ribbon

2 small sparkly, flower-shaped buttons

Tiny bunch of paper or silk flowers

Materials for basic bear, including pale beige double knitting (8 ply)

Crocheted Bears

Teddy bears have been around for over a hundred years and appeal to people of all ages. With this in mind, I have designed 20 tiny crocheted bears, each made from the same basic pattern and dressed in a different outfit. There's a keep-fit enthusiast, a gardener, a cook and an artist, to name just a few, and all the clothes and accessories can be easily adapted to make characters of your own.

Each little bear is approximately 4in (10cm) high and sits nicely in the palm of your hand. Though suitable for people of all ages, they are not, strictly speaking, playthings and are therefore not suitable for very young children and babies. They do, however, make unique and enduring gifts that your friends and family will treasure for many years to come.

The patterns are a little intricate in places but relatively simple to follow and, I am sure you will agree, the finished result will be well worth the effort.

Happy crocheting!

Basic crochet pattern

These are the instructions for making the basic crocheted bear. When working the pieces, it is a good idea to mark the beginning of each round to avoid losing or even gaining stitches.

Stuff each part with small amounts of filling as you work; avoid over-stuffing.

What you need

All the bears, their clothes and accessories are made using a size 2.50mm (US B-1, UK 13) crochet hook and a crisp no. 5 crochet cotton or, if you prefer, a fine fingering (4 ply) yarn. Two outfits – Ali the Baby Bear's clothes and Roz the Artist Bear's beret – use a no. 3 crochet cotton. Each bear will take approximately half a ball of crochet cotton in the main colour. For most of the clothes, features and accessories, oddments of yarn can be used. You will also need a small amount of fibrefill toy stuffing, and a darning needle for sewing up the bears and for the occasional piece of embroidery.

Measurements

Each bear measures approximately 4¼in (11cm) in height when sitting.

Tension/gauge

5 sc (*UK dc*) measure 1in (2.5cm) in width using the stated hook, though tension is not critical when making these bears if you are prepared to accept a small variation in size.

Instructions

Head

Row 1: with the appropriate colour yarn, make 2 ch, 6 sc (*UK dc*) in 2nd ch from hook, join in a circle with a sl st.
Row 2: 1 ch, 2 sc (*UK dc*) in each sc (*UK dc*) all round, join with a sl st [12 sts].
Rows 3–5: work in sc (*UK dc*).
Join the contrasting yarn, if stated in the instructions, and proceed as follows:
Row 6: *1 sc (*UK dc*) in next sc (*UK dc*), 2 sc (*UK dc*) in next sc (*UK dc*)*, rep from * to * all round.
Rows 7 and 8: work in sc (*UK dc*).
Row 9: inc 6 sc (*UK dc*) evenly in row.
Rows 10–15: work in sc (*UK dc*).
Row 16: dec 6 sc (*UK dc*) evenly in row.
Row 17: work in sc (*UK dc*).
Row 18: dec 6 sc (*UK dc*) evenly in row.
Row 19: work in sc (*UK dc*).

Row 20: dec 4 sc (*UK dc*) evenly in row.

Break yarn and run through last row. Draw up and fasten off.

Body

Row 1: with the appropriate colour yarn, make 2 ch, work 6 sc (*UK dc*) in 2nd ch from hook, join with a sl st to form a tight circle.

Subsequent rows are all joined with a sl st unless otherwise stated.

Row 2: 2 sc (*UK dc*) in each dc (*UK dc*) all round, join as before [12 sts].

Row 3: *1 sc (*UK dc*) in next st, 2 sc (*UK dc*) in next sc (*UK dc*)*, rep from * to * all round [18 sts].

Row 4: *1 sc (*UK dc*) in each of next 2 sc (*UK dc*), 2 sc (*UK dc*) in next sc (*UK dc*)*, rep from * to * all round [24 sts].

Row 5: *1 sc (*UK dc*) in each of next 3 sc (*UK dc*), 2 sc (*UK dc*) in next sc (*UK dc*)*, rep from * to * all round [30 sts].

Rows 6–18: sc (*UK dc*).

Row 19: dec 6 sts evenly all round [24 sts].

Row 20: sc (*UK dc*).

Rep rows 19 and 20 until 6 sc (*UK dc*) rem.

Finish stuffing the body, break yarn and run the thread through the last row. Draw up and fasten off.

Arms (make 2)

Row 1: with the appropriate colour yarn, make 2 ch, 7 sc (*UK dc*) in 2nd ch from hook, join in a tight circle with a sl st.

Row 2: 2 sc (*UK dc*) in each st, 14 sc (*UK dc*), join with a sl st.

Rows 3–14: sc (*UK dc*).

Row 15: *sc (*UK dc*) 2 tog, 1 sc (*UK dc*) in next sc (*UK dc*)*, rep from * to * all round.

Row 16: sc (*UK dc*) all round. Break yarn.

Complete the stuffing, pushing a little extra into the base of the arm to form the paw. Pull up to close. This is the top of the arm.

Legs (make 2)

The foot is shaped, so push a little extra stuffing into that area as you work.

Row 1: with the appropriate colour yarn, make 2 ch, 7 sc (*UK dc*) in 2nd ch from hook, join in a tight circle with a sl st.

Row 2: 2 sc (*UK dc*) in each st, 14 sc (*UK dc*), join with a sl st.

Row 3: *1 sc (*UK dc*), 2 sc (*UK dc*) in next st*, rep from * to *, working 1 sc (*UK dc*) in last st [20 sts].

Rows 4–6: sc (*UK dc*) all round.

Row 7: 7 sc (*UK dc*), [sc (*UK dc*) 2 tog] 3 times, 7 sc (*UK dc*).

Rows 8–17: sc (*UK dc*) all round.

Row 18: dec 3 sts evenly all round.

Row 19: sc (*UK dc*) all round.

Row 20: dec 3 sts evenly all round. Break yarn, draw yarn through last row of sc (*UK dc*), draw up and fasten off.

Ears (make 2)

Row 1: with the appropriate colour yarn, make 2 ch, 7 sc (*UK dc*) in 2nd ch from hook, join into a circle.

Row 2: 2 sc (*UK dc*) in each sc (*UK dc*) all round.

Row 3: sc (*UK dc*) all round. Fasten off.

To make up

Work in all the loose ends. Sew the head firmly to the body. You can position the head at different angles to give the bear more character. Pin the ears on each side of the head, and when you are happy with their position, sew them on firmly. Embroider the nose and eyes on to the head of the bear, then stitch a straight line from the centre of the nose to the chin, and a thin line above the eyes to make the eyebrows. Sew the arms in position on either side of the bear's shoulders. Attach the legs, one on each side, in a sitting position. Make sure they are level so that your bear sits down properly.

Party Mary

Make the bear following the basic instructions on pages 54–55, using ecru for the head, body, arms and legs and very light beige for the muzzle and ears.

Dress back

Row 1: Using red crochet cotton, make 21 ch, 1 sc (*UK dc*) in 2nd ch from hook, 1 sc (*UK dc*) in each ch to end, turn [20 sts].

Row 2: 1 ch, 1 sc (*UK dc*) in each sc (*UK dc*) to end, turn.

Row 3: rep row 2.

Row 4: sc (*UK dc*) 2 tog at each end of row [18 sts].

Row 5: sc (*UK dc*) to end.

Rows 6 and 7: rep rows 4 and 5 [16 sts].

Rows 8–10: sc (*UK dc*) to end.

Row 11: sl st across 3 sc (*UK dc*), work until 3 sc (*UK dc*) rem, turn.*

Work on these 10 sts for a further 8 rows. Fasten off.

Make frill along bottom edge of dress by working 2 dc (*UK tr*) in each st all along the starting chain. Fasten off.

Dress front

Work as dress back to *.

Continue on these sts for a further 4 rows.

Next row: work across 2 sc (*UK dc*), turn.

Continue on these 2 sts until strap matches back to shoulder. Fasten off.

Miss centre 6 sc (*UK dc*), join in yarn and complete to match other strap.

Work frill along bottom edge as for dress back.

To make up

Work the bear's features in brown floss. Sew the side seams of the dress. Take the sequin strip and measure enough to go all round the bottom of the dress. Stitch it in place along the last row of sc (*UK dc*), sewing through the centre of each sequin. Slip the dress on to the bear and sew the shoulder seams. Place the string of pearls around the bear's neck and tie it off firmly at the centre back of the neck. To make the headdress, wrap a piece of sequin strip around the bear's head, overlap it slightly at the back and stitch the two ends together. Take a tiny piece of marabou and stitch it to the join. Position the headdress on the bear's head and sew it in place with a few stitches. Cut a short length of the marabou to make a feather boa and drape it around the bear's neck.

What you need

Crochet hook size 2.50mm (US B-1, UK 13)

No. 5 crochet cotton – 1 ball of ecru, 1 ball of red

Small amount of crochet cotton in very light beige

Brown floss for embroidering features

Short strip of red sequins

Small piece of marabou in bright red

String of approx. 50 small pearl beads

Toy stuffing

Sewing needle and threads in colours to match crochet cotton

Sweet Angel

Make the bear following the basic instructions on pages 54–55, using pale blue for the head, body, arms and legs and mid blue for the muzzle and ears.

What you need

Crochet hook size 2.50mm (US B-1, UK 13)

No. 5 crochet cotton – 1 ball of pale blue

Small amounts of crochet cotton in mid blue, black, pale turquoise and white

Small amount of silver metallic yarn

Black floss for embroidering features

Short length of silver jewellery wire

Toy stuffing

Sewing needle and threads in colours to match crochet cotton

Wings (make 4)

Row 1: Using white crochet cotton, make 3 ch. 9 dc (*UK tr*) in 3rd ch from hook, turn.
Row 2: 3 ch, 1 dc (*UK tr*) in first dc (*UK tr*), 2 dc (*UK tr*) in each of rem dc (*UK tr*), turn.
Row 3: 1 sc (*UK dc*) in each dc (*UK tr*) to end.
Break white and join in metallic yarn. Work a further row of sc (*UK dc*) round the edge of the wing. Fasten off.

Skirt

Row 1: using pale turquoise, make 30 ch. Join with a sl st to beg of row, making sure you do not twist the chain.
Row 2: 1 ch, 1 sc (*UK dc*) in each ch to end, joining as before.
Row 3: 4 ch, miss 2 sc (*UK dc*), 1 sc (*UK dc*) in next sc (*UK dc*), *2 ch, miss 2 ch, 1 sc (*UK dc*) in next sc (*UK dc*)*. Rep from * to * all round, 2 ch, sl st to 2nd of 4 turning ch of previous row. Change to white yarn.
Row 4: sl st in first ch sp, 3 ch, [1 dc (*UK tr*), 2 ch, 2 dc (*UK tr*)] in same sp, *[2 dc (*UK tr*), 2 ch, 2 dc (*UK tr*)] in next sp*, rep from * to * all round, join in top of 3 ch at beg of row.
Row 5: rep row 4.
Row 6: change to pale turquoise and work row 5 again. Fasten off.

Join in metallic yarn and work edging as follows:
Row 7: *1 sc (*UK dc*) in each of next 2 dc (*UK tr*), picot in next sp, (3 ch, sl st in first of the 3 ch)*, rep from * to * all round, join with a sl st.

Halo

Row 1: Make 10 ch, join in a ring with a sl st, *5 ch, 1 sc (*UK dc*)*, rep from * to * 8 times, join with a sl st to beg of row.
Row 2: *5 sc (*UK dc*) in 5 ch loop, sl st in next sc (*UK dc*)*, rep from * to * all round, join with a sl st to beg of row. Fasten off.

To make up

Work in the ends on all the pieces. Sew the wings together in pairs. Join them in the centre and place them on the bear's back level with the tops of the arms. Sew them firmly in place. Slip the skirt on to the bear with the join at centre back. Secure with a few stitches. Take a length of silver jewellery wire and thread it around the inner edge of the halo. Twist the ends of the wire together and push them firmly in the bear's head towards the back. Arrange the halo in a pleasing shape.

Birthday Betsy

Make the bear following the basic instructions on pages 54–55, using light beige for the head, body, arms and legs and mid brown for the muzzle and ears.

Dress skirt

Row 1: using deep pink yarn, make 30 ch, join with a sl st to beg of row, making sure you do not twist the chain.

Row 2: 1 ch, 1 sc (*UK dc*) in each ch to end, joining as before.

Row 3: *3 ch, miss 1 sc (*UK dc*), 1 sc (*UK dc*) in next sc (*UK dc*)*, rep from * to * all round, join in 3 ch sp at beg of row.

Row 4: *3 ch, 1 sc (*UK dc*) in next 3 ch loop*, rep from * to * all round, joining as before.

Row 5: work as row 4.

Row 6: 3 ch, 4 dc (*UK tr*) in same loop as join, 5 dc (*UK tr*) in each following 3 ch loop, join with a sl st to top of 3 ch at beg of row. Fasten off.

Fold skirt in half with join at centre back.

Dress bodice

Row 1: working along starting ch, miss first 10 ch, join yarn into next ch, 1 sc (*UK dc*) in each of next 10 ch, turn.

Row 2: 1 ch, 1 sc (*UK dc*) in each sc (*UK dc*) to end, working last sc (*UK dc*) in place where yarn was joined in, turn.

Rows 3 and 4: sc (*UK dc*). Fasten off.

Crocheted flower for hat

Row 1: using deep pink yarn, make 4 ch, join in a circle with a sl st.

Row 2: *4 ch, 1 sc (*UK dc*) in circle*, rep from * to * 5 times, join with a sl st to beg of row. Fasten off.

To make up

Work in the ends on all the pieces. Make a chain long enough to reach from each corner of the bodice and around the bear's neck. Sew the chain to one corner of the bodice. Slip the dress on to the bear and secure the chain on the other side of the bodice. Sew a deep pink ribbon rose to the centre front of the dress. Thread the crystal beads on to a double length of strong thread to make the necklace. Tie the cotton firmly at the back of the bear's neck and secure. To make the hat, cut a small circle of pink net slightly bigger than the crocheted flower. Gather the circle slightly in the centre. Place the flower on top of the net, take three ribbon roses and place these in the centre of the flower. Now stitch through the roses, flower and net to hold them all together. Sew the hat to the top of the bear's head.

What you need

Crochet hook size 2.50mm (US B-1, UK 13)

No. 5 crochet cotton – 1 ball of light beige, 1 ball of deep pink

Small amounts of crochet cotton in mid brown

Black floss for embroidering features

4 tiny ribbon roses

Approx. 30 tiny crystal beads

Small piece of pink net for hat

Toy stuffing

Sewing needle and threads in colours to match crochet cotton

Wedding Kate

Make the bear following the basic instructions on pages 54–55, using cream and mid brown.

What you need

Crochet hook size 2.50mm (US B-1, UK 13)

No. 5 crochet cotton – 1 ball of cream

Small amounts of crochet cotton in mid brown

Black floss for embroidering features

Toy stuffing

Piece of cream net for veil, 2 x 3¼in (5 x 8cm)

7 small yellow and mauve paper roses

12 small white beads for collar

Sewing needle and threads in colours to match crochet cotton

Skirt

Row 1: using cream, make 30 ch, join with a sl st to beg of row, making sure you do not twist the chain.
Row 2: (RS) 1 ch, 1 sc (UK dc) in each ch to end, joining as before.
Row 3: 4 ch, miss 2 sc (UK dc), 1 sc (UK dc) in next sc (UK dc), *2 ch, miss 2 ch, 1 sc (UK dc) in next sc (UK dc)*, rep from * to * all round ending last rep, 2 ch, miss 2 ch, sl st in 2nd of 4 ch at beg of row.
Row 4: sl st in first ch sp, 3 ch, [1 dc (UK tr), 2 ch, 2 dc (UK tr)] in same sp, *[2 dc (UK tr), 2 ch, 2 dc (UK tr)] in next sp*, rep from * to * all round, join in top of 3 ch at beg of row.
Rows 5 and 6: rep row 4.
Turn, then work edging from WS: *1 dc (UK tr) in next st, sl st in next st*, rep from * to * all round, working in all sts and sps, join with a sl st to beg of row. Fasten off.

Crocheted flower for bouquet

Row 1: using cream yarn, make 8 ch and join in ring with a sl st.
Row 2: *4 ch, 1 sc (UK dc) in ring*, rep from * to * 5 times, join with a sl st.
Row 3: *[1 sc (UK dc), 1 dc (UK tr), 1 sc (UK dc)] in next 4 ch loop, sl st in next sc (UK dc)*, rep from * to * all round and join with a sl st to beg of row. Fasten off.

Crocheted flower for headdress

Row 1: using cream yarn, make 4 ch and join in a circle with a sl st.
Row 2: *4 ch, 1 sc (UK dc) in circle*, rep from * to * 5 times, join with a sl st to beg of row. Fasten off.

Collar

Row 1: using cream yarn, make 24 ch, 1 sc (UK dc) in 2nd ch from hook, 1 sc (UK dc) in each ch to end, turn.
Row 2: 1 ch, *sl st in next sc (UK dc), 1 dc (UK tr) in next sc (UK dc)*, rep from * to * along row. Fasten off.

To make up

For the headdress, use a needle and matching thread to gather the net across one short edge. Push two paper roses through the centre of the crocheted flower and twist the wire backs of the flowers together to secure them. Attach the gathered net to the crocheted headdress and arrange it on the bear's head. Secure with a few stitches. Take the collar and sew a tiny white bead to each point on the last row. Place the collar around the bear's neck and secure it at the centre back. For the bouquet, take five paper roses and arrange them in a neat bunch. Twist the wire backs together and thread them through the centre of the crocheted flower. Stitch the flowers to the crochet. Slip the skirt on to the bear with the join at the centre back and secure with a few stitches. Sew the bear's paws to the bouquet on each side.

Andy the Groom

Make the bear following the basic instructions on pages 54–55, using beige for the head, body, arms and legs and brown for the muzzle and ears.

Top hat crown
Row 1: using grey, make 2 ch, 6 sc (*UK dc*) in 2nd ch, join with a sl st.
Row 2: 2 sc (*UK dc*) in each sc (*UK dc*). Join with a sl st to beg of row.
Row 3: *1 sc (*UK dc*) in next sc (*UK dc*), 2 sc (*UK dc*) in next sc (*UK dc*)*, rep from * to * all round. Join as before. Fasten off.

Top hat side
Row 1: using grey, make 6 ch, 1 sc (*UK dc*) in 2nd ch from hook, 1 sc (*UK dc*) in each ch to end, turn.
Row 2: 1 sc (*UK dc*) into each sc (*UK dc*) to end, turn.
Continue on these 5 sts for a further 22 rows. Fasten off.

Hat brim
Row 1: using grey, make 27 ch, join in a circle with a sl st, making sure you do not twist the chain.
Row 2: 1 sc (*UK dc*) in each ch all round, join with a sl st to beg of row.
Row 3: 1 sc (1dc) in first sc (*UK dc*), *2 sc (*UK dc*) in next sc (*UK dc*), 1 sc (*UK dc*) in next sc (*UK dc*)*, rep from * to * all round, join as before.
Row 4: sl st in each sc (*UK dc*) all round. Fasten off.

To make up the top hat
Work in the ends on all the pieces. Take the side piece of the top hat and join the two short ends together to form a cylinder. Place the crown on to one end of the cylinder and stitch it carefully in place. Slip the brim over the hat, position it carefully and then stitch it in place. Take the ribbon and cut a piece to fit around the hat, leaving a tiny overlap. Stitch it in place. Catch the top hat to the bear's paw with a few stitches.

Waistcoat
Row 1: using black, make 30 ch, 1 sc (*UK dc*) in 2nd ch from hook, 1 sc (*UK dc*) in each ch to end.
Rows 2–4: work 3 rows sc (*UK dc*).
Row 5: work across 6 sc (*UK dc*), turn.
Row 6: work to last 2 sc (*UK dc*), sc (*UK dc*) 2 tog.
Row 7: sc (*UK dc*) 2 tog, work to end.
Row 8: work to last 2 sc (*UK dc*), sc (*UK dc*) 2 tog.
Row 9: sc (*UK dc*) 2 tog, work to end [2 sts].
Rows 10 and 11: work 2 rows sc (*UK dc*). Fasten off.
Rejoin yarn, miss 4 sc (*UK dc*), join to next sc (*UK dc*), work 10 sc (*UK dc*), turn and continue on these sts for back.
Work 8 rows sc (*UK dc*). Fasten off.
Next row: miss 4 sc (*UK dc*), rejoin yarn to rem sts and work other front to match, reversing shaping.

Cravat
Row 1: using cream, make 7 ch, 1 sc (*UK dc*) in 2nd ch from hook, 1 sc (*UK dc*) in each ch to end, turn.
Row 2: 1 ch, 1 sc (*UK dc*) in each sc (*UK dc*) to end, turn.
Rep row 2 until piece is 4¾in (12cm) long. Fasten off.

What you need

Crochet hook size 2.50mm (US B-1, UK 13)

No. 5 crochet cotton – 1 ball of beige

Small amounts of crochet cotton in black, brown and cream

Small amount of pale grey 4-ply yarn

Black floss for embroidering features

Small pearl bead for tie pin

1 yellow paper rose

Narrow satin ribbon in pale grey

Toy stuffing

Sewing needle and threads in colours to match crochet cotton

To make up the clothes
Tie the cravat around the
bear's neck, pouch slightly
and sew a pearl bead to the
centre to represent a tie pin.
Sew the shoulder seams on
the waistcoat and slip it on to
the bear. Arrange the cravat
under the waistcoat. Catch the
waistcoat together at the front
edge with a few stitches and
attach a paper rose. Personalise
your bear by attaching a
suitable button or charm to one
of his paws.

Dancing Bear

Make the bear following the basic instructions on pages 54–55, using mid blue for the head, body, arms and legs and light blue for the muzzle and ears.

Top hat crown

Row 1: using black yarn, make 2 ch, work 6 sc (*UK dc*) in 2nd ch, join with a sl st.

Row 2: 2 sc (*UK dc*) in each sc (*UK dc*). Join with a sl st to beg of row.

Row 3: *1 sc (*UK dc*) in next sc (*UK dc*), 2 sc (*UK dc*) in next sc (*UK dc*)*, rep from * to * all round and join as before. Fasten off.

Top hat side

Row 1: using black yarn, make 6 ch, 1 sc (*UK dc*) in 2nd ch from hook, 1 sc (*UK dc*) in each ch to end, turn.

Row 2: 1 sc (*UK dc*) in each sc (*UK dc*) to end, turn.

Continue on these 5 sts for a further 22 rows. Fasten off.

Brim of hat

Row 1: using black yarn, make 27 ch, join in a circle with a sl st, making sure you do not twist the chain.

Row 2: 1 sc (*UK dc*) in each ch, join with a sl st to beg of row.

Row 3: 1 sc (*UK dc*) in first sc (*UK dc*), *2 sc (*UK dc*) in next sc (*UK dc*), 1 sc (*UK dc*) in next sc (*UK dc*)*, rep from * to * all round, join as before.

Row 4: sl st in each sc (*UK dc*) all round. Fasten off.

Bow tie

Using white, make 26 ch, 1 sc (*UK dc*) in 2nd ch from hook, 1 sc (*UK dc*) in each ch to end. Fasten off.

Bow

Using white, make 5 ch, 1 sc (*UK dc*) in 2nd ch from hook, 1 sc (*UK dc*) in each ch to end.

Next row: 1 ch, 1 sc (*UK dc*) in each sc (*UK dc*) to end.

Rep last row 12 times. Fasten off.

Cane

With brown, make 20 ch, turn, 1 sc (*UK dc*) in 2nd ch from hook, 1 sc (*UK dc*) in each ch to end.

Fasten off.

To make up

Work in the ends on all the pieces. Take the side piece of the top hat and join the two short ends together to form a cylinder. Place the crown on to one end of the cylinder and stitch it carefully in place. Slip the brim over the hat, position it carefully then stitch it in place. Take the ribbon and cut a piece to fit around the hat, leaving a tiny overlap. Stitch it in place. Stuff the hat lightly and sew it in place on the bear's head. Take the bow and sew the two short ends together. Fold it in half with the join at the centre back. Run a thread through from top to bottom at the centre point and draw it up to form a bow shape. Sew the bow to the centre of the bow tie. Place it around the bear's neck and secure. Place the cocktail stick on to the piece of brown crochet and oversew the two sides together to enclose the wood. Snip off the two sharp points. Wind some metallic thread around one end of the stick to form the silver top. Glue it in place.

What you need

Crochet hook size 2.50mm (US B-1, UK 13) No. 5 crochet cotton – 1 ball of mid blue

Small amounts of crochet cotton in light blue, black and white

Black floss for embroidering features

Small amount of metallic yarn in silver

Cocktail stick

Small piece of narrow black satin ribbon for hat band

Toy stuffing

Craft glue

Sewing needle and threads in colours to match crochet cotton

Edward Bear

Make the bear following the basic instructions on pages 54–55, using mid brown for the head, body, arms and legs and dark brown for the muzzle and ears.

Waistcoat
Row 1: using mid blue, make 30 ch, 1 sc (*UK dc*) in 2nd ch from hook, 1 sc (*UK dc*) in each ch to end.
Rows 2–4: work 3 rows sc (*UK dc*).
Row 5: work across 6 sc (*UK dc*), turn.
Row 6: work to last 2 sc (*UK dc*), sc (*UK dc*) 2 tog.
Row 7: sc (*UK dc*) 2 tog, work to end.
Row 8: work to last 2 sc (*UK dc*), sc (*UK dc*) 2 tog.
Row 9: sc (*UK dc*) 2 tog, work to end [2 sts].
Rows 10 and 11: work 2 rows sc (*UK dc*). Fasten off.
Rejoin yarn, miss 4 sc (*UK dc*), join to next sc (*UK dc*), work 10 sc (*UK dc*), turn and continue on these sts for the back.
Work 8 rows sc (*UK dc*). Fasten off.
Miss 4 sc (*UK dc*), rejoin yarn to rem sts and work other front to match, reversing shaping.

Book covers (make 3, or any number you wish)
Row 1: using any colour you wish, make 8 ch, 1 sc (*UK dc*) in 2nd ch from hook, 1 sc (*UK dc*) in each ch to end, turn.
Row 2: 1 ch, 1 sc (*UK dc*) in each sc (*UK dc*) to end, turn.
Rep row 2 12 times. Fasten off.

Book pages (make 2 for large book; 1 for smaller books)
Row 1: using cream, make 7 ch, 1 sc (*UK dc*) in 2nd ch from hook, 1 sc (*UK dc*) in each ch to end, turn.
Row 2: 1 ch, 1 sc (*UK dc*) in each sc (*UK dc*) to end, turn.
Rep row 2 10 times. Fasten off.

To make up
Work in the ends on all the pieces. Join the shoulder seams on the waistcoat and slip it on to the bear. For the large, open book, place one set of pages on to a cover, and stitch it in place all round and down the centre. Attach another set of pages by sewing down the centre, then slightly fold the pages and catch them down on each side. For the closed books, fold a set of pages in half and lightly stuff before sewing them up. Place the pages inside a cover and fold the cover over, again catching in place around the outside edges. Using black floss or brown crochet cotton, embroider details on the spines and covers of the books.

What you need
Crochet hook size 2.50mm (US B-1, UK 13)

No. 5 crochet cotton – 1 ball of mid brown

Small amounts of crochet cotton in dark brown, light blue, mid blue, cream, yellow and green

Black floss for embroidering features

Toy stuffing

Sewing needle and threads in colours to match crochet cotton

Sparkles the Fairy

Make the bear following the basic instructions on pages 54–55, using mid pink for the head, body, arms and legs and dark pink for the muzzle and ears.

Wings (make 2)

Row 1: using gold metallic yarn, make 3 ch, 9 dc (*UK tr*) in 3rd ch from hook, turn.

Row 2: 3 ch, 1 dc (*UK tr*) in first dc (*UK tr*), 2 dc (*UK tr*) in each rem dc (*UK tr*), turn.

Row 3: 1 sc (*UK dc*) in each dc (*UK tr*) to end. Fasten off.

Skirt

Take the piece of net and fold it in half lengthwise, the folded edge forming the bottom of the skirt. Using a sewing needle and matching thread, lightly gather the net to fit around the bear's waist. Secure the thread firmly to ensure the skirt remains gathered.

Using pink crochet cotton, work a row of sc (*UK dc*) along the top edge of the skirt, working through both thicknesses of net.

Turn, and work a further row of sc (*UK dc*). Fasten off.

Headdress

Using metallic yarn, make 4 ch, join in a circle with a sl st.

Next row: *4 ch, 1 sc (*UK dc*) in circle*, rep from * to * 5 times, join with a sl st to beg of row. Fasten off.

To make up

Make the wand by wrapping the cocktail stick tightly with a length of metallic yarn, leaving a small section at one end uncovered to enable you to stick on the star. Secure the ends of the yarn with craft glue. Take two adhesive stars and press them together firmly, one on each side of the top of the stick. Secure the wand in the bear's paw by threading it through the crochet stitches. Sew the wings together firmly at the centre. Place them in the middle of the bear's back and secure. Sew small sequin stars randomly over the net skirt. Place the skirt around the bear's waist and sew the crochet band together at the centre back. Finally, work in the ends of the crocheted headdress and attach an adhesive star firmly to the centre. Sew the headdress to the top of the bear's head with some tiny stitches.

What you need

Crochet hook size 2.50mm (US B-1, UK 13)

No. 5 crochet cotton – 1 ball of mid pink

Small amount of crochet cotton in dark pink

Small amount of gold metallic yarn

Dark brown floss for embroidering features

Toy stuffing

7 small sequin stars

Piece of pink net for skirt, 7 x 4¾in (18 x 12cm)

Cocktail stick

3 adhesive gold, sparkly stars

Sewing needle and threads in colours to match crochet cotton

Craft glue

Keep-fit Mazzy

Make the bear following the basic instructions on pages 54–55, using beige for the head and legs, lilac for the body and ecru for the muzzle and ears. For each arm, work the first 10 rows in beige, then change to lilac and complete the rest of the arm.

Leg warmers (make 2)
Row 1: using dark pink, make 18 ch, 1 dc (*UK tr*) in 3rd ch from hook, 1 dc (*UK tr*) in each ch to end, turn.
Row 2: 3 ch, miss 1 dc (*UK tr*), 1 dc (*UK tr*) in each dc (*UK tr*) to end.
Row 3: rep row 2.
Row 4: 1 ch, 1 sc (*UK dc*) in each dc (*UK tr*) to end. Fasten off.

Head band
Using dark pink, make 30 ch, break pink and join in lilac, work 1 sc (*UK dc*) in 2nd ch from hook, 1 sc (*UK dc*) in each ch to end, break lilac and turn.
Join in dark pink, sl st in each sc (*UK dc*) to end. Fasten off.

Sports bag, front and back
Row 1: using dark pink, make 13 ch, 1 sc (*UK dc*) in 2nd ch from hook, 1 sc (*UK dc*) in each ch to end, turn.
Row 2: 1 ch, 1 sc (*UK dc*) in each sc (*UK dc*) to end, turn.
Repeat row 2 18 times. Fasten off.

Bag handles (make 2)
Using black, make 18 ch.
Fasten off.

Bag strap
Using black, make 38 ch.
Fasten off.

Arm bands (make 2)
Using dark pink, make 18 ch.
Fasten off.

Neck band
Using dark pink, make 30 ch.
Fasten off.

To make up
Sew the arm bands on to the arms, where the colour changes from beige to lilac. Arrange the neck band around the bear's neck so that it is scooped slightly at the front, and attach it to the body with one or two small stitches. Join the head band in a circle and place it on the bear's head. Secure with a few tiny stitches. Take the main piece of the sports bag, fold it in half and sew the side seams. Stuff it lightly with a little stuffing to give it shape and close the top. Sew a handle to either side of the bag and attach the strap at either end. Fold the leg warmers in half lengthways and sew the side seam. Slip them on to the bear's legs.

What you need
- Crochet hook size 2.50mm (US B-1, UK 13)
- No. 5 crochet cotton – 1 ball of beige
- Small amount of crochet cotton in ecru, black, lilac and dark pink
- Toy stuffing
- Black floss for embroidering features
- Sewing needle and threads in colours to match crochet cotton

Belinda Butterfly

What you need

Crochet hook size 2.50mm
(US B-1, UK 13)

No. 5 crochet cotton – 1 ball
of white

Small amounts of crochet cotton in
beige, dark brown and light blue

Black and yellow floss for
embroidering features
and butterfly

Tiny paper flowers in yellow
and pink

Tiny pale blue ribbon bow

Toy stuffing

Sewing needle and threads in
colours to match crochet cotton

Make the bear following the basic
instructions on pages 54–55, using
white for the head, body, arms and
legs and beige for the muzzle
and ears.

Skirt

Row 1: using light blue, make 30
ch, join with a sl st to beg of row,
making sure you do not twist
the chain.
Row 2: 1 ch, 1 sc (UK dc) in each
ch to end, joining as before.
Row 3: 4 ch, miss 2 sc (UK dc), 1
sc (UK dc) in next sc (UK dc), *2 ch,
miss 2 ch, 1 sc (UK dc) in next sc
(UK dc)*, rep from * to * all round,
2 ch, sl st to 2nd of 4 turning ch of
previous row.
Row 4: *3 ch, 1 sc (UK dc) in next
3 ch loop*, rep from * to * all round,
joining as before.
Row 5: as row 4.
Row 6: [1 sc (UK dc), 2 dc (UK tr), 1
sc (UK dc)] in each 3 ch loop. Join
with a sl st to beg of row. Fasten off.

Basket

Row 1: using dark brown, make
3 ch, 14 dc (UK tr) in 2nd ch from
hook, join with a sl st.
Row 2: 2 dc (UK tr) in each dc (UK
tr) all round. Join as before.
Row 3: working into back loop of
stitch only, 1 dc (UK tr) in each st to
end, join as before.
Work 2 rows of sc (UK dc).
Fasten off.

Basket handle

Using dark brown, make 20 ch, 1 sc
(UK dc) in 2nd ch from hook, 1 sc
(UK dc) in each ch to end.
Fasten off.

Butterfly

Using light blue, make 2 ch, 3 dc
(UK tr) in 2nd ch from hook, 1 sl st
in same place, 3 ch, 3 dc (UK tr) in
same place, 1 sl st in same place, 3
ch, 3 dc (UK tr) in same place, sl st
in same place, 3 ch, 3 dc (UK tr) in
same place, sl st in same place and
fasten off. Sew the centre together
to form four wings.

To make up

Work in the ends on all the pieces.
Attach the tiny blue ribbon bow to
the bear's head. Slip the skirt on to
the bear with the join at the centre
back. Add a tiny amount of stuffing
to the basket to give it a rounded
shape and sew one end of the
handle on to each side. Wire the
flowers together into a neat bunch,
place them inside the basket and
secure them with a few a stitches.
Shape the butterfly's wings, then
take some yellow floss and sew
a tiny spot on to each wing using
French knots. Use some black floss
to work the body in straight stitches.
Fray the end of the black floss to
make antennae. Sew the butterfly to
the bear's paw.

Gardening Bear

Make the bear following the basic instructions on pages 54–55, using beige for the head, body and arms and dark brown for the muzzle and ears. For the legs, work using mid green, then join in light blue at row 8 and work rows 8, 10 and 12 in light blue.

Apron

Row 1: using mid green, make 17 ch, 1 dc (*UK tr*) in 4th ch from hook, 1dc (*UK tr*) in each ch to end, turn.
Row 2: 1 ch, 1 sc (*UK dc*) in each sc (*UK dc*) to end, turn.
Row 3: 3 ch, miss 1 dc (*UK tr*), 1 dc (*UK tr*) in each dc (*UK tr*) to end.
Row 4: 1 ch, 1 sc (*UK dc*) in each dc (*UK tr*) to end, turn.
Rows 5 and 6: rep rows 3 and 4.
Row 7: sl st over 4 dc (*UK tr*), 3 ch, 1 dc (*UK tr*) in each st to last 3 dc (*UK tr*), turn.
Row 8: 3 ch, dc (*UK tr*) 2 tog, work to last 3 sts, dc (*UK tr*) 2 tog, 1 dc (*UK tr*) in top of turning ch of previous row.

Pocket

Row 1: using dark green, make 10 ch, 1 sc (*UK dc*) in 2nd ch from hook, 1 sc (*UK dc*) in each ch to end, turn.
Row 2: 1 ch, 1 sc (*UK dc*) in each sc (*UK dc*) to end, turn.
Rows 3 and 4: rep row 2.
Fasten off.

Spade – blade

Row 1: using metallic yarn, make 7 ch, 1 sc (*UK dc*) in 2nd ch from hook, 1 sc (*UK dc*) in each ch to end, turn.
Row 2: 1 ch, 1 sc (*UK dc*) in each sc (*UK dc*) to end, turn.

Repeat last row 12 times. Fasten off.

Spade – shaft

Row 1: using dark brown, make 12 ch, 1 sc (*UK dc*) in 2nd ch from hook, 1 sc (*UK dc*) in each ch to end, turn.
Row 2: 1 ch, 1 sc (*UK dc*) in each sc (*UK dc*) to end, turn.
Row 3: rep row 2. Fasten off.

Spade – handle

Row 1: using dark brown, make 8 ch, 1 sc (*UK dc*) in 2nd ch from hook, 1 sc (*UK dc*) in each ch to end, turn.
Row 2: 1 ch, 1 sc (*UK dc*) in each sc (*UK dc*) to end, turn.
Row 3: rep row 2. Fasten off.

To make up

Work in the ends on all the pieces. Sew the pocket to the front of the apron. Using green yarn, make a chain long enough to go round the bear's neck, then attach the top of the apron at each corner. Make two short lengths of chain as ties for the apron and attach one on each side. Put the apron on to the bear and tie the apron at the back. Fold the blade part of the spade in half lengthwise and stitch the sides together. Fold the shaft lengthways into a tight oblong and stitch it firmly. Do the same with the handle. Stitch the handle to the shaft, then attach the shaft to the blade. Stitch the fork and trowel on to the pocket.

What you need

Crochet hook size 2.50mm (US B-1, UK 13)

No. 5 crochet cotton – 1 ball of beige and 1 ball of mid green

Small amounts of crochet cotton in dark brown, mid brown, light blue and dark green

Black floss for embroidering features

Small amount of metallic yarn in silver

2 tiny plastic flowers, card fork and trowel

Toy stuffing

Sewing needle and threads in colours to match crochet cotton

Flower pot

Row 1: using dark brown, make 2 ch, 6 sc (*UK dc*) in 2nd ch from hook, join in a circle with a sl st.

Row 2: 1 ch, 2 sc (*UK dc*) in each sc (*UK dc*) all round, join as before.

Rows 3–7: 1 ch, 1 sc (*UK dc*) in each st, join as before.

For the soil, use dark brown and make 3 ch, 6 sc (*UK dc*) in 2nd ch from hook, join in a circle. Work 2 sc (*UK dc*) in each st all round, join and fasten off.

Lightly stuff the flower pot to give it shape. Put the soil inside the pot and catch it in place. Push the two plastic flowers through the centre of the soil and secure with a few stitches.

Caroline the Cook

Make the bear following the basic instructions on pages 54–55, using yellow and mid brown.

Apron
Row 1: using pale pink, make 15 ch, 1 dc (*UK tr*) in 4th ch from hook, 1 dc (*UK tr*) in each ch to end, turn.
Row 2: 1 ch, 1 sc (*UK dc*) in each sc (*UK dc*) to end, turn.
Row 3: 3 ch, miss 1 dc (*UK tr*), 1 dc (*UK tr*) in each dc (*UK tr*) to end.
Row 4: 1 ch, 1 sc (*UK dc*) in each dc (*UK tr*) to end, turn.
Rows 5 and 6: rep rows 3 and 4.
Row 7: sl st over 4 dc (*UK tr*), 3 ch, 1 dc (*UK tr*) in each st to last 3 dc (*UK tr*), turn.
Shape waist:
Row 8: 3 ch, dc (*UK tr*) 2 tog, work to last 3 sts, dc (*UK tr*) 2 tog, 1 dc (*UK tr*) in top of turning ch of previous row.
Row 9: sc (*UK dc*) 2 tog, work to last 2 sts, sc (*UK dc*) 2 tog, turn.
Row 10: 1 sc (*UK dc*) in each of next 3 sts, turn. Work the strap:
Row 11: 1 sc (*UK dc*) in next st, sc (*UK dc*) 2 tog, turn.
Work in sc (*UK dc*) on these 2 sts until strap is long enough to go round bear's neck and will reach to the other corner of the apron bib.
Fasten off.

Apron edging
Row 1: using mid pink, join yarn to one side of waist. Work sc (*UK dc*) all round apron to other side of waist, turn.
Row 2: 1 ch, *1 sc (*UK dc*) in next st, 1 dc (*UK tr*) in next st*, rep from * to * all round edge. Fasten off.

Apron ties (make 2)
Row 1: using pale pink, make 17 ch, 1 sc (*UK dc*) in 2nd ch from hook, 1 sc (*UK dc*) in each ch to end, turn.
Row 2: 1 ch, 1 sc (*UK dc*) in each st to end. Fasten off.

Pocket
Row 1: using mid pink, make 8 ch, 1 sc (*UK dc*) in 2nd ch from hook, 1 sc (*UK dc*) in each ch to end, turn.
Row 2: 1 ch, 1 sc (*UK dc*) in each sc (*UK dc*) to end, turn.
Rows 3 and 4: rep row 2. Fasten off.

Apples (make 5)
Using green, make 3 ch, work 9 dc (*UK tr*) in 2nd ch from hook, break yarn and run end through each st.

Pie top
Row 1: using light beige, make 2 ch, 6 sc (*UK dc*) in 2nd ch from hook, join in a circle with a sl st.
Row 2: 1 ch, 2 sc (*UK dc*) in each st to end, join as before.
Row 3: 1 ch, [1 sc (*UK dc*) in next st, 2 sc (*UK dc*) in next st] to end, join.
Row 4: 1 ch, [1 sc (*UK dc*) in each of next 2 sts, 2 sc (*UK dc*) in next st] to end, join.
Row 5: 1 ch, [1 sc (*UK dc*) in each of next 3 sts, 2 sc (*UK dc*) in next st] to end, join.
Row 6: 1 ch, *1 dc (*UK tr*) in next st, 1 sc (*UK dc*) in next st*, rep from * to * all round, join with a sl st. Fasten off.

Pie base
Work as for pie top, but omit the last row.

What you need
Crochet hook size 2.50mm (US B-1, UK 13)

No. 5 crochet cotton – 1 ball of yellow

Small amounts of crochet cotton in mid brown, dark brown, light beige, green, pale pink and mid pink

Black floss for embroidering features

Toy stuffing

Sewing needle and threads in colours to match crochet cotton

Basket

Row 1: using dark brown, make 3 ch, 14 dc (*UK tr*) in 2nd ch from hook, join with a sl st.

Row 2: 2 dc (*UK tr*) in each dc (*UK tr*) all round, join as before.

Row 3: working into back loop of st only, work 1 dc (*UK tr*) into each dc (*UK tr*) to end, join.

Work 2 rows of sc (*UK dc*). Fasten off.

Using dark brown, make 10 ch for each handle. Fasten off.

To make up

Work in the ends on all the pieces. Sew the top of the pie to the base, adding a tiny piece of stuffing as you do so. Shape it into a pie shape. For each leaf on top of the pie, use light beige to make 5 ch. Form each chain into a tiny loop and sew them to the centre of the pie top. To make the apron, work in the ends on all the pieces. Sew the pocket to the centre front of the apron and attach one tie to each side at the waist. Put the apron on to the bear, pass the strap round the bear's neck and stitch it in place to the other side of the bib. Sew the handles to the sides of the basket. Draw the green chains up to form tight balls, adding a tiny piece of stuffing as you do so, close and secure. Thread a short length of dark brown through the top of each apple to make a stalk. Place the apples inside the basket.

Rozzy the Artist

Make the bear following the basic instructions on pages 54–55, using pale yellow for the head, body, arms and legs, dark brown for the ears and beige for the muzzle.

Sleeves (make 2)
Row 1: using light blue, make 17 ch, 1 dc (*UK tr*) in 3rd ch from hook, 1 dc (*UK tr*) in each ch to end, turn.
Row 2: 3 ch, miss 1 st, 1 dc (*UK tr*) in each st to end.
Rows 3 and 4: rep row 2.
Row 5: 1 ch, 1 sc (*UK dc*) in each st to end. Fasten off.

Smock (make 2)
Row 1: using light blue, make 20 ch, 1 dc (*UK tr*) in 3rd ch from hook, 1 dc (*UK tr*) in each ch to end, turn.
Row 2: 3 ch, miss 1 st, 1 dc (*UK tr*) in each dc (*UK tr*) to end.
Row 3: 3 ch, miss 1 st, dc (*UK tr*) 2 tog, dc (*UK tr*) to last 3 sts, dc (*UK tr*) 2 tog, 1 dc (*UK tr*) in last st.
Row 4: sl st across next 4 dc (*UK tr*), 3 ch, 1 dc (*UK tr*) in each dc (*UK tr*) to last 3 dc (*UK tr*), turn.
Row 5: 3 ch, 1 dc (*UK tr*) in each st to end.
Row 6: 3 ch, 1 dc (*UK tr*), 1 hdc (*UK htr*), 5 sc (*UK dc*), 1hdc (*UK htr*), 2 dc (*UK tr*). Fasten off.

Beret
Row 1: using navy blue, make 30 ch, 1 sc (*UK dc*) in 2nd ch from hook, 1 sc (*UK dc*) in each ch to end, join with a sl st into a circle.
Rows 2 and 3: sc (*UK dc*) all round, join as before.
Row 4: 1 ch, *1 sc (*UK dc*) in next sc (*UK dc*), 2 sc (*UK dc*) in next sc (*UK dc*)*, rep from * to * all round, join as before.

Rows 5 and 6: sc (*UK dc*) all round, join as before.
Row 7: 1 ch, *sc (*UK dc*) 2 tog, 1 sc (*UK dc*) in next st*, rep from * to * all round, ending last rep sc (*UK dc*) 2 tog, join as before.
Row 8: sc (*UK dc*) all round.
Row 9: 1 ch, *sc (*UK dc*) 2 tog, 1 sc (*UK dc*) in next st*, rep from * to * all round, ending last rep sc (*UK dc*) 2 tog, join as before.
Row 10: sc (*UK dc*) all round.
Row 11: 1 ch, *sc (*UK dc*) 2 tog, 1 sc (*UK dc*) in next st*, rep from * to * all round, ending last rep 1 sc (*UK dc*) in each of last 2 sts, join as before.
Row 12: sc (*UK dc*) all round.
Break yarn and run the thread through each sc (*UK dc*) all round. Draw up and fasten off. Make a tiny loop and attach to the top of the beret.

Palette
Row 1: using white, make 9 ch, 1 sc (*UK dc*) in 2nd ch from hook, 1 sc (*UK dc*) in each ch to end, turn.
Rows 2–6: 1 ch, 1 sc (*UK dc*) in each ch to end.
Do not fasten off but continue along 1 short end as follows:
Row 7: 1 sc (*UK dc*) in next 2 row ends, 2 ch, miss 2 row ends, 1 sc (*UK dc*) in last 2 row ends, turn.
Row 8: 1 ch, sc (*UK dc*) to end, working 2 sc (*UK dc*) in space made on previous row. Fasten off.
Take 8 different coloured beads and sew in place on the palette to represent paint colours.

What you need:

Crochet hook size 2.50mm (US B-1, UK 13)

No. 5 crochet cotton – 1 ball of pale yellow and 1 ball of light blue

Small amounts of crochet cotton in mid brown, dark brown, beige, navy blue (no. 3) and white

Dark brown floss for embroidering features, and green and yellow floss for embroidery on easel

Tiny coloured beads for paint palette

6 cocktail sticks, 5 with one blunt end and 1 with two blunt ends.

Toy stuffing

Sewing needle and threads in colours to match crochet cotton

Easel

Using mid brown, make a ch the same length as a cocktail stick. Work 3 rows of sc (*UK dc*) on this chain, fasten off. Wrap the crochet piece lengthways around the stick and oversew it in place firmly. The point should be visible at one end. Repeat this on a further three cocktail sticks, including the one with two blunt ends.

Canvas

Row 1: using white, make 15 ch, 1 sc (*UK dc*) in 2nd ch from hook, 1 sc (*UK dc*) in each ch to end, turn.
Rows 2–14: 1 ch, 1 sc (*UK dc*) in each ch to end, turn. Fasten off. Embroider a flower on to the front of the canvas using yellow and green floss.

To make up

Work in the ends on all the pieces. Catch the back and front smock pieces at the shoulder edges, just enough to hold them together. Stitch the sleeves in place. Sew the side and sleeve seams. Put the smock on to the bear and sew the shoulder seams on either side. Place the beret on the side of the bear's head and secure with a few stitches. Place the palette on the bear's paw and stitch it in place. Take two cocktail sticks and flatten the sharp end of each slightly to split the wood and create a brush effect. Place the brushes into the thumb hole on the palette and secure with some tiny stitches. Now assemble the easel. First make an A frame by stitching together the top part of two sticks, then sew the stick with two blunt ends horizontally across the centre to create the 'A'. Secure a fourth stick at the back of the frame so that the easel will stand up. Oversew the top of the three upright sticks together firmly. Place the canvas centrally on to the cross bar of the easel and sew it in place.

Musical Briony

Make the bear following the basic instructions on pages 54–55, using beige for the head, body, arms and legs and mid brown for the muzzle and ears.

Accordion – bellows

Row 1: using black, make 18 ch, 1 sc (*UK dc*) in 2nd ch from hook, 1 sc (*UK dc*) in each ch to end, turn.
Row 2: 1 ch, 1 sc (*UK dc*) in each st to end, working into back loops only.
Rep row 2 until you have 6 ridges on either side. Fasten off.

Accordion – button section

Row 1: using red, make 9 ch, work 1 sc (*UK dc*) into 2nd ch from hook, 1 sc (*UK dc*) in each ch to end, turn.
Rows 2–10: 1 ch, 1 sc (*UK dc*) in each st to end, turn.
Fasten off.

Accordion – keyboard section

Work in two parts – one as the button section (above), and the other in the same way but repeating row 10 twice before fastening off. For the keys, use white to make 3 ch, 1 sc (*UK dc*) in 2nd ch from hook, 1 sc (*UK dc*) in last st, turn and work sc (*UK dc*) on these 2 sts for a further 8 rows. Fasten off.

Strap

Using brown make 18 ch. Fasten off.

Collar

Row 1: using white, make 25 ch, work 1 sc (*UK dc*) in 2nd ch from hook, 1 sc (*UK dc*) in each ch to end, turn.

Row 2: 4 ch, miss 2 sts, 1 sc (*UK dc*) in next st, *2 ch, miss 2 sts, 1 sc (*UK dc*) in next st*, rep from * to * to end.
Row 3: 1 ch, *2 sc (*UK dc*) in first st, sl st in next sc (*UK dc*)*, rep from * to * ending last rep, sl st in top of turning ch of previous row. Fasten off.

To make up

Work in the ends on all the pieces. Place the collar around the bear's neck, with the opening at the centre front, and stitch it in place. Sew a French knot into the centre of the flower using yellow floss. The accordion is assembled in three pieces. Take the button section and fold it lengthwise into a tight oblong. Sew along the sides. Embroider eight tiny French knots on to one side using white floss (follow the picture opposite for guidance). For the keyboard section, fold both parts into tight oblongs and place one behind the other so that the longer part sits at the back – from the side, it will have an L shape. Sew these parts together. Take the keys and sew them on to one side (again, refer to the photograph). Use black floss to embroider on the black keys. Take the bellows section and fold it in half so that the ridges are vertical. Sew along the two short ends and base, putting a tiny amount of stuffing into the piece before closing. Attach the keyboard and button sections to the bellows. Attach a strap to the buttons end of the accordion and place it over the bear's arm.

What you need

Crochet hook size 2.50mm (US B-1, UK 13)

No. 5 crochet cotton – 1 ball of beige

Small amounts of crochet cotton in mid brown, dark brown, red, black, white and green

Black floss for embroidering features, yellow floss for flower centre and white floss for embroidery on accordion

Toy stuffing

Sewing needle and threads in colours to match crochet cotton

Flower

Using red, make 3 ch and join into a circle with a sl st. *3 ch, 1 sc (*UK dc*) in circle*, rep from * to * 5 times. Fasten off.

Leaf

Using green, make 5 ch, 1 sc (*UK dc*) in 2nd ch from hook, 1 hdc (*UK htr*) in each of next 2 ch, 1 sc (*UK dc)* in last ch. Work along other side of starting ch in same way, join with a sl st.

Attach the flower to the leaf and stitch them on the bear's head beside one ear.

Bernie the Elf

Make the bear following the basic instructions on pages 54–55, using beige for the head, body, arms and legs and dark brown for the muzzle and ears.

Sleeves

Row 1: using red, make 17 ch, 1 dc (*UK tr*) in 3rd ch from hook, 1 dc (*UK tr*) in each ch to end, turn.
Rows 2–4: 3 ch, miss 1 st, 1 dc (*UK tr*) in each st to end.
Row 5: 1 ch, 1 sc (*UK dc*) in each st to end. Fasten off.

Tunic (make 2)

Row 1: using red, make 20 ch, dc (*UK tr*) in 3rd ch from hook, 1 dc (*UK tr*) in each ch to end, turn.
Rows 2 and 3: 3 ch, miss 1 st, 1 dc (*UK tr*) in each dc (*UK tr*) to end.
Row 4: 3 ch, miss 1 st, dc (*UK tr*) 2 tog, dc (*UK tr*) to last 3 sts, dc (*UK tr*) 2 tog, 1 dc (*UK tr*) in last st.
Row 5: sl st across next 4 dc (*UK tr*), 3 ch, 1 dc (*UK tr*) in each dc (*UK tr*) to last 3 dc (*UK tr*), turn.
Row 6: 3 ch, dc (*UK tr*) in each st to end.
Row 7: 3 ch, 1 dc (*UK tr*), 1 hdc (*UK htr*), 5 sc (*UK dc*), 1 hdc (*UK htr*), 2 dc (*UK tr*). Fasten off.

Collar

Using green, make 24 ch, 1 sc (*UK dc*) in 2nd ch from hook, dc (*UK tr*) 2 tog over next 2 ch. Fasten off.
*Rejoin yarn to next ch, dc (*UK tr*) 2 tog over next 2 ch. Fasten off.* Rep from * to * along rest of ch, ending 1 sc (*UK dc*) in last ch.

Hat

Row 1: using green, make 26 ch, 1 sc (*UK dc*) in 2nd ch from hook, 1 sc (*UK dc*) in each ch to end, turn.
Row 2: 1 ch, 1 sc (*UK dc*) in each st to end, turn.
Rows 3 and 4: changing to red, 3 ch, miss 1 st, 1 dc (*UK tr*) in each st to end, turn.
Rows 5 and 6: 3 ch, miss 1 st, dc (*UK tr*) 2 tog across row to last st, 1 dc (*UK tr*) in last st, turn.
Rows 7 and 8: 3 ch, 1 dc (*UK tr*) in each st to end.
Row 9: 3 ch, dc (*UK tr*) 2 tog 3 times, 1 dc (*UK tr*) in last tr, turn.
Row 10: 3 ch, miss 1 dc (*UK tr*), 1 dc (*UK tr*) in each st to end.
Break yarn.
Run thread through last row, draw up and secure.

Belt

Using green, make ch long enough to go round the bear's waist with a little extra for overlap. Fasten off.

To make up

Work in the ends on all the pieces. Catch the back and front tunic pieces at the shoulder edges to hold them in place. Stitch the sleeves in place. Sew the side and sleeve seams and put the tunic on to the bear. Sew the shoulder seams on either side. Sew the seam on the hat and attach three tiny gold beads to the point. Place the belt around the bear's waist and catch the ends together at the centre back. Place the collar around the bear's neck and join at the centre back. Stretch it slightly to give a good fit.

What you need

Crochet hook size 2.50mm (US B-1, UK 13)

No. 5 crochet cotton – 1 ball of beige and 1 ball of red

Small amounts of crochet cotton in dark brown and mid green

Black floss for embroidering features

3 tiny gold beads for hat

Toy stuffing

Sewing needle and threads in colours to match crochet cotton

Panda Paul

Make the bear following the basic instructions on pages 54–55, using black for the ears, arms and legs and white for the head. For the body, work the first 9 rows in white and the remainder in black.

Eye patches (make 2)

Row 1: using black, make 2 ch, 6 sc (UK dc) in 2nd ch from hook, join in a circle with a sl st.

Row 2: 2 sc (UK dc) in each sc (UK dc) all round, join with a sl st.

Row 3: 1 sc (UK dc) in each of next 4 sc (UK dc). Fasten off.

Bamboo shoot

Row 1: using brown, make 12 ch, 1 sc (UK dc) in 2nd ch from hook, 1 sc (UK dc) in each ch to end, turn.

Row 2: sc (UK dc) to end. Fasten off.

Green leaves (make 3)

Using green, make 5 ch. Fasten off.

To make up

Work in the ends on all the pieces, leaving a long tail on the end of each leaf. Place the eye patches on either side of the head, pull them into an oval shape and sew in place. Using black floss, make a French knot in the centre of each eye patch to make the eyes. Fold the brown section of the bamboo in half lengthways and sew it together firmly. Take a leaf strand and run the long thread down into the top of the brown stem. Secure it with one or two tiny stitches. Repeat with the remaining leaves. Sew the bamboo shoot to the palm of the panda's paw, and catch the other paw to the shoot to look as though the panda is holding it.

What you need

Crochet hook size 2.50mm (US B-1, UK 13)

No. 5 crochet cotton – 1 ball of black and 1 ball of white

Small amounts of crochet cotton in mid brown and mid green

Black floss for embroidering features

Toy stuffing

Sewing needle and threads in colours to match crochet cotton

Flamenco Juan

Make the bear following the basic instructions on pages 54–55, using beige for the head, body, arms and legs and dark brown for the muzzle and ears.

Hat

Row 1: using black, make 2 ch, 6 sc (*UK dc*) in 2nd ch from hook, join this row and all subsequent rows with a sl st to form a circle.
Row 2: 2 sc (*UK dc*) in each sc (*UK dc*) all round [12 sts].
Row 3: inc 4 sc (*UK dc*) evenly all round [16 sts].
Rows 4–7: sc (*UK dc*) all round.
Row 8: 2 sc (*UK dc*) in each sc (*UK dc*) to end [32 sts].
Rows 9 and 10: sc (*UK dc*), inc 6 sts evenly on each row [44 sts].
Row 11: sc (*UK dc*).
Row 12: 1 sl st in each st round brim. Join and fasten off.

Hat band

Using red, make a chain long enough to fit around the crown of the hat. Work 1 row of sc (*UK dc*) along the chain. Fasten off.

Bandana

Row 1: using red, make 2 ch, 2 sc (*UK dc*) in 2nd ch from hook, turn.
Row 2: 1 ch, 1 sc (*UK dc*) in each st to end, turn.
Rows 3–7: sc (*UK dc*), inc 1 st at each end of row until there are 12 sc (*UK dc*).
Row 8: work 1 sc (*UK dc*) in each of next 2 sts, turn.
Rows 9–16: continue in sc (*UK dc*) on these 2 sts. Fasten off.
Miss centre 8 sts, rejoin yarn and complete to match other side.

Guitar – neck

Row 1: using mid brown, make 15 ch, work 1 sc (*UK dc*) in 2nd ch from hook, 1 sc (*UK dc*) in each ch to end, turn.
Rows 2 and 3: sc (*UK dc*).
Fasten off.

Guitar – body, top (make 2)

Row 1: using mid brown, make 2 ch, 6 sc (*UK dc*) in 2nd ch from hook, join with a sl st.
Row 2: 2 sc (*UK dc*) in each sc (*UK dc*) all round, join with a sl st.
Fasten off.

Guitar – body, bottom (make 2)

Work as top to end of row 2.
Row 3: *1 sc (*UK dc*) in next st, 2 sc (*UK dc*) in next st*, rep from * to * all round. Fasten off.

Guitar – side

Using dark brown, make a ch long enough to fit all round the outside edge of the guitar body.
Work 1 dc (*UK tr*) in 3rd ch from hook, 1 dc (*UK tr*) in each ch to end. Fasten off.

Rose

Using red, make 3 ch, join into a circle with a sl st.
Work *3 ch, 1 sc (*UK dc*) into circle*, rep from * to * 5 times. Fasten off. Gather the base of the flower to form a rose.
Using green, make 7 ch to form the stem. Thread green into a needle and work two loops on either side of stem to form tiny leaves.
To finish, attach the stem to the rose and pull the stem through the bear's muzzle using a crochet hook.

What you need

Crochet hook size 2.50mm (US B-1, UK 13)

No. 5 crochet cotton – 1 ball of beige

Small amounts of crochet cotton in black, red, dark brown, mid brown, green and white

Black floss for embroidering features

Toy stuffing

Sewing needle and threads in colours to match crochet cotton

To make up

Work in the ends on all the pieces. Sew the hat band around the hat. Position the hat on the bear's head and sew it in place. Using white yarn, embroider French knots all over the bandana in random spots. Tie the bandana around the bear's neck. Fold the guitar neck lengthwise into a neat oblong and oversew it firmly together. For the guitar body, sew one top and one bottom section together for the front, and repeat for the back. Carefully pin the side of the guitar around the outer edge of either the front or back of the body, then sew it in place. Take the other part of the guitar body and stitch this to the side in the same way, leaving a small opening at the top. Push a small amount of stuffing into the guitar body, shape it, then insert the neck into the opening and secure with a few stitches. Using black yarn, sew lengths of thread on to the front of the guitar to represent strings. Secure them at the top and bottom. Make two French knots on each side of the head to represent the pegs.

Sophie Swimmer

Make the bear following the basic instructions on pages 54–55, using pale yellow for the head, body, arms and legs and beige for the muzzle and ears.

Swimsuit

Row 1: using black, make 11 ch, 1 sc (*UK dc*) in 2nd ch from hook, 1 sc (*UK dc*) in each ch to end, turn.
Rows 2 and 3: 1 ch, 1 sc (*UK dc*) in each sc (*UK dc*) to end, turn.
Rows 4–6: inc 1 sc (*UK dc*) at each end of row until there are 16 sc (*UK dc*).
Rows 7–9: sc (*UK dc*).
Row 10: sl st over 3 sc (*UK dc*), sc (*UK dc*) to last 3 sc (*UK dc*), turn.
Row 11: sc (*UK dc*).
Rows 12–13: dec 1 sc (*UK dc*) each end of row until there are 6 sc (*UK dc*).
Rows 14–21: work 8 rows sc (*UK dc*).
Rows 22–23: inc 1 sc (*UK dc*) at each end of row until there are 10 sc (*UK dc*).
Row 24: sc (*UK dc*) to end, make 4 ch, turn.
Row 25: 1 sc (*UK dc*) in 2nd ch from hook, 1 sc (*UK dc*) in each sc (*UK dc*) to end, make 4 ch, turn.
Row 26: repeat row 25.
Rows 27–29: sc (*UK dc*).
Rows 30–32: dec 1 sc (*UK dc*) at each end of row until there are 10 sc (*UK dc*).
Rows 33–34: work in sc (*UK dc*).
Row 35: 2 sc (*UK dc*), turn.
Work in sc (*UK dc*) on these 2 sts until strap is long enough to fit over bear's shoulder to back of swimsuit. Fasten off.

Miss centre 6 sc (*UK dc*), rejoin yarn to rem 2 sts and work to match other strap. Fasten off.

Towel

Row 1: using white, make 15 ch, 1 sc (*UK dc*) in 2nd ch from hook, 1 sc (*UK dc*) in each ch to end, turn.
Row 2: 1 hdc (*UK htr*) in each st to end, turn.
Rows 3 and 4: join in blue and work sc (*UK dc*).
Rows 5 and 6: pick up white and work hdc (*UK htr*).
Rows 7 and 8: pick up blue and work sc (*UK dc*).
Row 9: pick up white and work hdc (*UK htr*).
Row 10: sc (*UK dc*). Fasten off.

To make up

Work in the ends on all the pieces. Sew up the side seams of the swimsuit and slip it on to the bear. Take the straps over the bear's shoulders and sew them on to either side of the costume at the back. Embroider a tiny motif in white on the front.

What you need

Crochet hook size 2.50mm (US B-1, UK 13)

No. 5 crochet cotton – 1 ball of pale yellow

Small amounts of crochet cotton in black, beige, blue and white

Black floss for embroidering features

Toy stuffing

Sewing needle and threads in colours to match crochet cotton

Pink Baby Bear

Make the bear following the basic instructions on pages 54–55, using pale pink for the head, body, arms and legs and salmon pink for the muzzle and ears.

What you need

Crochet hook size 2.50mm (US B-1, UK 13)

No. 5 crochet cotton – 1 ball of pale pink

Small amounts of crochet cotton in white and salmon pink

Small amount of no. 3 crochet cotton in mid pink for clothes

3 pale pink ribbon-and-rose bows

Tiny pink safety pin

Brown floss for embroidering features

Toy stuffing

Sewing needle and threads in colours to match crochet cotton

Bootees (make 2)

Row 1: using mid pink, make 8 ch, 1 dc (*UK tr*) in 2nd ch from hook, 1 dc (*UK tr*) in each st to last ch, 5 dc (*UK tr*) in last ch, do not turn. Continue along other side of starting ch. Work 1 dc (*UK tr*) in each st to last ch, 4 dc (*UK tr*) in last ch, join with a sl st to beg of row. This completes the sole.
Rows 2 and 3: 2 ch, 1dc (*UK tr*) in each dc (*UK tr*) all round, join with a sl st to beg of row.
Row 4: sc (*UK dc*).
Row 5: 3 ch, miss 1 sc (*UK dc*), 1 dc (*UK tr*) in next sc (*UK dc*), *1 ch, miss 2 sc (*UK dc*), 1 dc (*UK tr*) in next sc (*UK dc*)*, rep from * to * to end of row, sl st into beg of row.
Row 6: 3 ch, 2 dc (*UK tr*) in first ch sp, 1 sc (*UK dc*) in next ch sp, *3 dc (*UK tr*) in next ch sp, 1 sc (*UK dc*) in next ch sp*, rep from * to * all round, join to base of first dc (*UK tr*) at beg of row. Fasten off.

Diaper/nappy

Row 1: using white yarn, make 36 ch, 1 sc (*UK dc*) in 2nd ch from hook, 1 sc (*UK dc*) in each ch to end, turn.
Row 2: 1 ch, 1 sc (*UK dc*) in each ch to end, turn.
Rows 3–17: dec 1 sc (*UK dc*) at each end of row until 1 sc (*UK dc*) rem. Fasten off.

Top

Row 1: using mid pink, make 32 ch, 1 sc (*UK dc*) in 2nd ch from hook, 1 sc (*UK dc*) in each ch to end.
Row 2: 4 ch, miss 2 sc (*UK dc*), 1 dc (*UK tr*) in next st, *1 ch, miss 1 sc (*UK dc*), 1 dc (*UK tr*) in next st*, rep from * to * to end. Fasten off.

For left back, work along starting ch as follows:
Row 1: 1 sc (*UK dc*) in each of next 6 ch, turn.
Row 2: sc (*UK dc*) 2 tog, sc (*UK dc*) to end, turn.
Rows 3–5: sc (*UK dc*).
Row 6: 3 sc (*UK dc*), turn.
Rows 7–9: sc (*UK dc*). Fasten off.
Return to main piece and continue working along starting ch for front.
Row 1: miss 3 ch, join yarn to next ch, work 1 sc (*UK dc*) in same place as join, 1 sc (*UK dc*) in each of next 13 ch [14 sts].
Row 2: sc (*UK dc*) 2 tog, sc (*UK dc*) to last 2 sts, sc (*UK dc*) 2 tog.
Rows 3–5: sc (*UK dc*).
Shape neck:
Row 6: work across 3 sc (*UK dc*), turn.
Rows 7–9: sc (*UK dc*). Fasten off.
Miss centre 6 sc (*UK dc*), rejoin yarn to next sc (*UK dc*), 1 sc (*UK dc*) in next 3 sc (*UK dc*), turn and complete right back to match left back, reversing shaping instructions. Fasten off.
Work to match first side of neck. Fasten off.
Join shoulder seams.
Work edging along bottom:
Join yarn to top of first dc (*UK tr*), 3 ch, 2 dc (*UK tr*) in first ch sp, *1 sc (*UK dc*) in next sp, 3 dc (*UK tr*) in next sp*, rep from * to * to end. Fasten off.

To make up

Work in the ends on all the pieces. Join the centre back seam of the top, slip it on to the bear, and join the shoulder seams. Sew a ribbon-and-rose bow to the front of the top. Sew a ribbon-and-rose bow to the centre front of each bootee and slip the bootees on to the bear's feet. Fold the diaper/nappy around the bear, tuck the end over the centre section and secure with a tiny safety pin.

Sunshine Susie

Make the bear following the basic instructions on pages 54–55, using dark brown for the head, body, arms and legs and beige for the muzzle and ears.

Honey pot
Row 1: using light brown, make 2 ch, 6 sc (*UK dc*) in 2nd ch from hook. Join in a circle with a sl st.
Row 2: 2 sc (*UK dc*) in each sc (*UK dc*) all round.
Row 3: *1 sc (*UK dc*) in next sc (*UK dc*), 2 sc (*UK dc*) in next sc (*UK dc*)*, rep from * to * all round.
Rows 4–6: working into back loops of sts only, 1 hdc (*UK htr*) in each sc (*UK dc*) all round, join with a sl st.
Row 7: *2 hdc (*UK htr*), hdc (*UK htr*) 2 tog*, rep from * to * to last 2 hdc (*UK htr*), 1 hdc (*UK htr*) in each of next 2 hdc (*UK htr*).
Rows 8 and 9: 1 sc (*UK dc*) in each hdc (*UK htr*) all round. Fasten off.

Honey-pot lid
Work rows 1–3 of pot, run thread up into centre of lid, make a large French knot on top of the lid to form the handle.

Honey
Using gold, work rows 1–3 of honey pot. Fasten off.

Label
Row 1: using beige, make 6 ch, 1 sc (*UK dc*) in 2nd ch from hook, 1 sc (*UK dc*) in each ch to end.
Rows 2–5: 1 sc (*UK dc*) in each sc (*UK dc*) to end, turn.
Fasten off.

Bees – body (make 2)
Row 1: using yellow, make 2 ch, 4 sc (*UK dc*) in 2nd ch from hook, join in a circle.
Rows 2–4: 1 sc (*UK dc*) in each sc (*UK dc*) all round, join.
Rows 5 and 6: join in black, work as rows 2–4, break yarn. Thread yarn through needle, draw up top of bee, sew through to make head.

Bees – wings (make 2)
Using white, make 6 ch, work 1 sl st in first ch, 5 ch, sl st in same place again. This forms two tiny loops. Fasten off, leaving long threads.

To make up
Work in the ends on all the honey-pot pieces. Stuff the honey pot lightly to give it a rounded shape. Slip the honey inside the top of the pot and sew it in place. Sew the label to the front of the honey pot and, using black floss, embroider the word 'honey' across the centre of the label. Stitch the honey-pot lid to the bear's paw, as shown opposite. Push the ends on each bee's body inside the body to lightly pad it. Stitch black lines around the body to form stripes using embroidery floss. Use the long threads on the wings to secure them to the bees' bodies. Work the ends through to the other side of the body and use them to secure one bee to the side of the honey pot and the other to the bear's shoulder.

What you need
Crochet hook size 2.50mm (US B-1, UK 13)

No. 5 crochet cotton – 1 ball of dark brown

Small amounts of crochet cotton in beige, mid brown, white, yellow, gold and black

Black floss for embroidering features, and details on honey pot and bees

Toy stuffing

Sewing needle and threads in colours to match crochet cotton